INTRODUCTION X

Recent Titles from smith|doorstop

The Poetry Business publishes pamphlets and collections under the smith|doorstop imprint, children's poetry under the small|donkey imprint and pamphlets from young poets as part of The New Poets List, together with *The North* magazine. Recent publications include:

Pamphlets:
Stephen Knight, *A Swansea Love Song*
Julie Mellor, *Out of the Weather*
Matt Black, *Spoon Rebellion*
The International Book & Pamphlet Competition 2017 Winners:
Josephine Abbott, Katy Evans-Bush, Ruth McIlroy and Lesley Saunders

small|donkey:
Carole Bromley, *Blast Off!*
Dean Parkin, *The Bubble Wrap*

The New Poets List:
Theophilus Kwek, *The First Five Storms*
Jenny Danes, *Gaps*
Phoebe Stuckes, *Gin & Tonic*

Anthologies:
CAST: The Poetry Business Book of New Contemporary Poets
Thirty at Thirty: Celebrating 30 years of smith|doorstop pamphlets
One for The Road: A Pub Anthology

Order the above titles now from the shop at
http://www.poetrybusiness.co.uk

INTRODUCTION X

The Poetry Business Book of New Poets

Edited by
Suzannah Evans & Peter Sansom

smith|doorstop

Published 2017 by
smith|doorstop books
The Poetry Business
Bank Street Arts
32-40 Bank Street
Sheffield S1 2DS
www.poetrybusiness.co.uk

ISBN 978-1-910367-99-5

All rights reserved. No part of this publication may be reproduced or transmitted in any form or by any means, electronic or mechanical, including photocopy, recording, or any information storage and retrieval system, without permission in writing from the publisher.

British Library Cataloguing-in-Publication Data.
A catalogue record for this book is available from the British Library.

Typeset by Utter

Cover design by Utter
Printed and bound by CPI Group (UK) Ltd, Croydon, CR0 4YY

smith|doorstop books is a member of Inpress, www.inpressbooks.co.uk. Distributed by NBN International, Airport Business Centre, 10 Thornbury Road Plymouth PL 6 7PP.

The Poetry Business receives financial support from
Arts Council England.

Contents

LYDIA ALLISON
    Vivian 11
    Romance 12

LAURA ATTRIDGE
    Wolf 13
    The Visit 14
    Autumn in New Jersey 15

HELEN BOWELL
    Coming from the Mill 16
    23 June 17

LEWIS BROWN
    Tsukumogami 18

IAN BURNETTE
    Introduction X 19
    High Noon 20
    A Boy is a Gun 21

JOHN-PAUL BURNS
    The Minute of Vision 22
    Deliveroo 23
    The Owl 24
    Monday on Saturday 25

KATIE BYFORD
    Galatea 26
    Wax and Water 28

IMOGEN CASSELS
    Christopher 30
    The Bat 32
    Flora 33

JENNY DANES
    Gaps 34
    Shower 35
    Deutsch 36
    Notes on missing a person 37

JEI DEGENHARDT
    Sonnet – house party 38
    Glaukós 39

KYM DEYN
    Dog Violets 40

LOUISE ESSEX
    Half head 41
    Cancer 42
    Oysters 43

SARAH FLETCHER
    Wives and Girlfriends 44
    Christina Crashes The Wedding 45
    The Occupant 46
    Fragments/Campari 47

ELIZABETH GIBSON
    Old rain 48
    Eden 49
    Going 50

JAMES GIDDINGS
    Popsicle 51
    Instead of You Here 52
    In another life 53

SARAH GONNET
    Psychosomatic 54
    The Girl Who Lived in a House Made of Books 55

JESSICA HANSON
    Possibly 57
    Enough Water To Drown 58

LIZZI HAWKINS
    Kissing the geographer 59
    Train poem 60
    Winter poem 62

KATHERINE HENDERSON
    Coal 63
    Amber 64
    Daily devotion 65

KATHERINE HORREX
    Polycystic 66
    Parliament, Fallen 67

LYDIA HOUNAT
    Some Of Us Do Not Have Freckles 68
    this is what it feels like 69

SIAN HUGHES
    Gannet 70

HANA KAPETANOVIC
    A Scenic Moment 71
    How To: Romance 72
    The continuity of substance 73

GREGORY KEARNS
    Pneumatophore 75
    Spacemen 76
    Expedition 77
    123 Cherry Tree Lane 78

SAFIA KHAN
    Grandma's Kitchen 79
    Umma's Room 80
    Home 81

STEFAN KIELBASIEWICZ
    Five-a-day 82
    of a Salesman 84

THEOPHILUS KWEK
    The First Five Storms 87

DOMINIC LEONARD
    Nightmare 90
    To a Back, 2am 91

THEODORA OYANI
    Dawn 93

LAURA POTTS
    Ancestors 94
    Merrie City 96

FIELDING RONSHAUGEN
    Aeolian Processes 97
    Sarah Good 99
    Celia and Rosalind 100

ALEXANDER SHAW
    Landscape without Reiver 101
    Occupation 102
    How to Prepare for Bad News 103

JASMINE SIMMS
    St Chad 104
    Hitching 105
    Recurring Dream 107
    School 108

PHOEBE STUCKES
    Home 109
    Crisis 110
    Judgement 111

SOPHIE TURNER
    Ursa Major 112
    The Far Side of the Moon 113

ELOISE UNERMAN
    I Saw Myself 114
    Glass 115

CHARLOTTE WETTON
    In Mexico 116
    Home Safe 117
    Bident 118

JESSICA WOOD
Dorveille: 119
Fragments   120

YUAN YANG
Silk shirt   121
Dog Eat Dog   122
Routine   124

WARDA YASSIN
My sisters   125
The Hijab   126
Making Lips   127

RUTH YATES
Strawberries   128
Bird Gift   129
Playing in the Snow   130

Index of poems & first lines   132
Acknowledgments   141

Introduction X

Is a gathering of outstanding poets at an early stage in their writing careers. Most are in their early twenties (some in their teens), and though many have appeared in magazines and five or six have pamphlets to their name, all are relatively new to publishing.

Apart from this 'newness', and talent, and what W S Graham would call 'the rarer gift of application', what these writers happen to have in common is that at some point The Poetry Business has been fortunate enough to encounter them. This was either through residential courses, The New Poets Prize, or workshops and mentoring. The latter is by far the largest slice of the pie chart, especially through the Writing Squad, for which Peter Sansom has been an associate tutor and The Poetry Business a valued resource for over a decade.

The Writing Squad is rigorous though imaginative in its recruitment and offers a serious and in-depth programme of support and development across all writing genres – something which is evident in much of the poetry collected here. And, since the Squad draws together young writers living or studying in the North, with meetings in Manchester, Sheffield and Newcastle, there is also a geographical bias, and perhaps this, as much as the younger perspective, is reflected in some of the subject matter here and its treatment.

Even so, *Introduction X* includes writing from around the country and further afield (Singapore for instance, and the US), and it has benefitted especially from the wide-ranging sympathies of Andrew McMillan and Helen Mort, both of whom have been instrumental in The Poetry Business's New Poets Prize, with Helen also being a key member of the Writing Squad team.

In addition, there are writers that Ann and Peter S have been impressed by on Arvon or other courses and in among submissions for *The North* magazine. Suzannah Evans, assistant editor at the PB and co-editor of this book, has brought a keen eye to the selection process as well as in some cases helping Peter to shape some of the individual poems. Nevertheless, there are doubtless dozens of excellent younger poets whom between us we have managed to overlook. Who knows, perhaps there will be an expanded *X* a year or two down the line. For now, though, it only remains to thank various members of the Writing Squad for their editorial input also and not least its Director, Steve Dearden. The Poetry Business is proud and delighted to publish this extraordinary and exciting anthology.

LYDIA ALLISON

Lydia Allison is a Sheffield-born poet, fascinated with names and the people behind them. She is a graduate of the Writing Squad and is currently studying for an MA in Poetry at Manchester Metropolitan University. She has appeared both online and in print, links at lydiaallison.com

Vivian

After the first time,
we didn't laugh the way we did before
at the battered Jag, their poor
attempts at getting wrecked. Good wine
at breakfast, or with cake. Ice
in cider for the pleasure of it. Mortal
fear of homosexuality, a decade over,
cat-calls about dying.

Alone, I read the book,
his name was Vivian. He died.
I saw the need we sometimes have
to record a life. His looks,
his style, things he said
to the wolves; reciting Hamlet.

Romance

makes me feel like strawberries
as if my skin
makes water fragrant

my taste bright on your lips
as you slice away
stars of leaves. As you say

*you're my favourite
thing*, take the fruit, dab
pink stains in sugar.

LAURA ATTRIDGE

Laura Attridge is a poet, librettist and playwright hailing from Yorkshire and based in London. She is founder and Artistic Director of opera and theatre company And So Forth. Previous publication includes *The Rialto* and *Mslexia*, and her song cycles have been premiered at Glyndebourne, the National Gallery, the Royal College of Music (RCM), and Bard College, New York. Recent and upcoming works for the stage include *Now* (RCM/Tête-à-Tête Festival), *Damsel/Wife/Witch* (And So Forth), *P.U.C.K.* (RCM), *Belongings* (Glyndebourne), *A Mind Lively* (Helios Collective) and *Then to the elements* (Scottish Opera).

Wolf
    from *'Damsel/Wife/Witch'*

'There,' he says, pointing, 'there, see?'

A cluster of flowers in the curve of a tree-root.
In the falling light his eyes are brighter
than petals: they glint.

'Look,' he says, 'look, lean closer.'

A hand-tailored tuxedo covers his pelt;
it cannot cover the smell of earth,
of damp grey mushrooms.

He takes off his gloves, and gently brushes
the constellation of freckles
on my pale forearm.

'There,' he says, 'perfect for picking.'

His hands are unexpectedly human.
It is dusk and he has kissed me.

The Visit
after Don Paterson

One night last summer
I was lying in your bed, sleepless,
limbs flung out from under the duvet
to escape the heat of your embrace,
when Love stepped quietly into the house.

He came up the staircase,
hesitated in the hallway, one foot
pressing an uneven floorboard.
The bedroom door was ajar; seeing me,
my skin to the heat, he nudged his way in.

'Not now,' I whispered,
drawing the bedclothes up to my chin,
but he started pulling items, one by one,
from my open suitcase, haphazardly
discarding things around the room.

You stirred, murmured
into my neck, made signs of waking,
pulled my ever-alert body towards you.
He slipped out of the open window,
leaving two odd socks draped over the sill.

I lay, wondering
what strange ritual this was
that I had witnessed, listening
to your heavy, regulated breaths,
anticipating nothing, something, everything.

Autumn in New Jersey

The autumns of my childhood are best:

Avenues are lined with all the words
you can think of for red, yellow, orange, gold.

The neighbourhood kids
ride bikes through drifts.

Raking: a dullness in my lower back,
the unexpected damp in the middle of the pile.

Smell of decay.
We wash our hands clean of the cling of it,
but it persists in sweaters and socks.

Trees are taking off their gloves in the park;
ballgames become rare.

At school, we hear again about the Pilgrims,
dig out last year's costumes
for which we are now a year too tall.

In the ever-earlier dusk, the vivid leaves tremble.
I carry their richness with me.

Laura Attridge

HELEN BOWELL

Helen is a poetry editor at *The Cadaverine*, and a member of the Dead [Women] Poets Society, a project exploring women poets' relationships to women writers of the past. In 2010 and 2011, she was a commended Foyle Young Poet. She graduated from an English Literature degree at Durham in 2016, where she edited the literary magazine *From the Lighthouse* and was president of the Creative Writing Society. She has been published in *The Manchester Review* and *The Missing Slate*. She is Education Co-Ordinator for the Poetry Society.

Coming from the Mill

Close to midnight, we finish the puzzle
we bought from the Arndale. For the first time
since you told me, we try drowning the silence with kissing.
It's a jigsaw of a Lowry painting, and it's pretty tough
because all those half-bent spines and hats coming
from the mill look the same. I touch your hand,
you touch my lips, parting them like lifting the top
off the jigsaw box: smooth, well-worn, easy.
It bothers me how hard it is, all those people
being the same but slightly different, enough
to make it clear you'd messed up after six or seven pieces,
but never to tell exactly where. I wrinkle your clothes
into the floor, deciding it's easier to shuffle on
than guess who else has done the same.

The jigsaw wakes me in the night. I can't stop wondering
if we pushed some of the pieces in the wrong places
and never noticed, imposing on families displaced faces,
lost arms, broken legs, severing siblings clean in half,
it bothers me for hours, until I have to get out of bed and check,

and find you've tidied it away
and laid out the puzzle for tomorrow evening's game.

23 June

David, I don't feel like kissing tonight.
The news has got me down and I know
we need each other now, more than ever,
but when I'm asleep and dreaming it off
I'll be thumbing my way to Dover
in any lorry that'll take me.
So can we just lie tonight, cross-armed,
on our own sides of the bed,
and try to sleep, listening to the city's
long, withdrawing roar?

LEWIS BROWN

Lewis Brown is a performance poet and reformed prose writer from sunny Northumberland. He writes mostly fantasy and horror, in a very broad sense, and is a very keen gamer. He keeps a poetry blog at fallingpiano.wordpress.com

Tsukumogami*

Oh, they will try to keep it from you.
Your hand-me-downs and heirlooms
Grand pianos and second-hand hairbrushes
would rather you didn't know
that when you weren't looking, they scraped together souls of their own
from discarded feelings, memories and morning rituals and
the songs you sang while using them.

Grandfather clocks may keep their own time
chairs will sometimes stretch their legs
and pictures will look kindly on the ones their likeness loved
as the glass covering them becomes rose-tinted.

Don't get too nostalgic, though –
– it's not all favorite armchairs and swing sets.
Just as the bed that made a marriage may hold you close
your mirror might wonder what it's doing wrong
when you curse your own reflection
and god knows what your diary thinks of you
of itself.

Sometimes I rise in the morning
and everything I own is alive
my alarm clock, judging me for another late start
my thermos, asking if it's going to be another late night
my toothbrush, telling me I don't do this often or well enough
my phone reminding me I'm just a call away from not alone.
That's the thing about possessions:
you can't help but be honest with them.
Like children, they learn by association
and take everything to heart.

*Any household object which, having reached its 100th birthday, becomes self-aware.

IAN BURNETTE

Ian Burnette is from Pittsburgh, Pennsylvania. His poems have appeared in *Best New Poets 2015*, *The Forward Book of Poetry*, *the Kenyon Review*, and elsewhere, and he is an associate at *the Kenyon Review* and a senior at Kenyon College. He lives in central Ohio.

Introduction X
after Terrance Hayes

I am in love with reversal. How a room is just a moor
      looking the other way, or a moor in a doom mood
           as it locks a liquored wanderer beneath the heather.

Gink nus, sun king, pin snip, pools sloop. I can't make
      heads or tails of noon, her face of perfect symmetry.
           Somewhere, not here, if you pull a dead girl from the river

and hang her on a drying line, you can bring her
      back to life. Somewhere, the mystery is not what will
           come in the night but how to put the body back together.

Dog god, drib bird, ate eta. It's almost like words,
      the body, same symmetry and violence. What I touch
           turns to gold. What I touch turns to dust. The blue wire

is connected to the blue wire. The red wire wants to drown all in its sight.

High Noon

It's true, sometimes
        only the horses survived.
Not even a hold-up man would put holes in a stallion
that might later carry him.

A town drains through the floorboards,
        its center soundless.
        The mare, caparisoned with blood,
bows to drink from the bath.

A Boy is a Gun

Strange, how over and over again the west is won.
I used to wake up a person, but now I wake up a gun.
A masked man holds me like the woman he loves.

We ride in a Cadillac the color of licorice. It hums
and shines in the sun, its whisper like religion.
Strange, how over and over again the west is won

by the glow of the twenty dollar bill, the motion
of cargo in the night. Beneath a medicine-blue sky
the masked man holds me like the woman he loves

behind a house bathed in search-light. He works
a bullet inside me with the edge of his thumb.
Strange, how over and over again the west is won

and not won. How I am first the match and then
the fire, and then the match that set the house ablaze.
The masked man holds me. Like the woman he loves

I am already asleep and deep in a dream as explicit as
something red and damned and lying on the ground.
Strange, how over and over again the west is won.
A masked man holds me like the woman he loves.

Ian Burnette

JOHN-PAUL BURNS

John-Paul Burns was born in Manchester in 1991. He has published poems in *The North* and *Poetry Salzburg Review* and is a Creative Writing MfA student at Manchester Metropolitan University.

The Minute of Vision

it has come, here, in Castle Market
at nine-thirty-eight in the morning
of the switching climates, in the morning
of warm rain and bright but mild sun,
in the land of the pink-booted lady
who passes a lit joint to a gum-chewing lad
who seems surprised but takes it
in his stride, here beside Argos, here
the place of ambiguously sticky stains
and ambiguously sticky stares from these
the bloodshot-bearded eyes, the day-drinkers
and the dvd-merchants, their cases speckled
with dusty raindrops, second-hand smoke
smiles from the crooked prams and worn wheels
for now, the time of the one-handed
mate-yelling bmxer has come, the time of his swerving,
the time of the merging scents and ways.

Deliveroo

I shoot along smooth tarmac
with lobster risotto
in a box on my back
I ring Huang-Lee Mun
He comes in silken pyjamas
He may know it's almost two
he may not
He may have lobster risotto each day
for breakfast
or for lunch

The Owl
after Edward Thomas

I was walking up Northumberland Road,
knackered from the rush, the streaming
from concert to bookshop, workshop & cinema –
some such soul-enriching nonsense anyway.

It's a special kind of city-tired
when your blood feels grey and your eyes
double-glazed on the sill of your brain –
struggling up the hill again – the Owl

its voice from the oak, from the poplar
from the cherries as I turn onto Glebe Road –
almost home and the Owl knows it –
how it loves to mark the deep-green night

Not Yours to all who pass, *Not Yours* –
the street mammals and I go slow and cold –
Not Yours again, and me, *I Know* – silence –
It swoops off unseen – Our noise spreads out again.

Monday on Saturday

Saturday, it's time to grow up.
Sleeping all week, holding out
for your limelight to come
has left you sloppy, tired
and you talk absolute nonsense.

Saturday, putting all your hopes
in one basket over and over again,
the grass is always greener
when it's growing on you.

I'm sorry Saturday, but time's up.
The wrinkle has come,
the hunt is over.

Your eyes are bloodshot with bags
and your laughter is brittle

as a pint glass.

John-Paul Burns

KATIE BYFORD

When not in Durham studying for the final year of her Classics degree, Katie Byford is in London moonlighting as a poet and dabbling in other art forms. She was a member of the Barbican Young Poets from 2011 to 2014 and was before commended in the Foyle Young Poets competition and the Young Poets on the Underground competition. She has had work published in *Magma* and by Bloodaxe, and has been a member of the Burn After Reading collective since 2012, through them working with institutions such as South Bank University and the Wellcome Collection. Katie has been a member of the Writing Squad since beginning her studies in the North East, and has in the past year set up an arts platform, Thorn, which holds regular events and publishes poetry and other art forms online.

Galatea

He drew me up from the water. When drowning,
you may have enough time to observe the light
on the surface, how it reaches tentatively into dimples
and grooves and how the waxy glass melts in its hands.
When he drew me up my skin was soaked white like milk
my eyes were closed and both my lungs were full
to my collarbone. When drowning you may have time
to contemplate the nature of cold: a baby swathed
in its folds, you will see yourself curl, clench
into stillness like a fist, feel your limbs saturate
and solidify. When drowning you may be conscious
as never before of the red clay, that fiery creature
shot from the flint of your teeth; how it writhes
and withers in your jaw, extinguished.
He slung my body onto the bank with a dull dmmft
like marble on soft pillows. When drowning you learn
that vanity is really all that a dead body can expect
to convey to the living – vanitas, emptiness –
all except for the lover, who will convince himself
that his kiss, his hands, his cries of love
will bruise you back to life,
where you will remain for him. When drowning
you may learn that to grow cold is perhaps
the only thing we have for ourselves. He might now learn
that he prefers you sweaty-palmed,
cracked-lipped, greasy-haired
– not this taut skin, this hard flesh
which does not yield and flutter to his touch;

that he prefers you graceless, awkward,
bickering, selfish, tactless
and alive. When drowning
you hope that he
will shape you into
yourself again
with words, with
poetry, before
your brain
becomes a
stone
in his lap.

Wax and Water

i.

Your cells collapse
gracefully, like Alexandria
into the sea.

Barnacles cling to your fingers
and ossify your grip
into crab legs.

Lunch is a silent mass
of Greek philosophers huddled about fires
suddenly mute with nothing to say.
You ask why they are serving
gravy with the main course
and not with pudding.

ii.

You tell us sometimes
that everything hurts
as if it's a secret.
You cannot kneel,
so receive the host in bed.
They feed crackly communion wafers
through the speaker at your headboard
between stacking people in pews
and cleanup on bed 25.

iii.

A forest leans its forehead
against your window,
mocking your arthritidigits.
They can no longer paint the leaves.

iv.

His picture sits
beside you, in the place
he used to take at home. There are some things,
you say, so tender that they cannot hurt.

v.

You tell us
that the soul is oil
floating on water
or the flame
burning still on a pillar
of drooping wax,

and then you smile
in a lighthouse kind of way, as if
to let us know
what light still shines
through your translucent skin.

IMOGEN CASSELS

Imogen Cassels is from Sheffield, and studies in Cambridge. In 2015 she was a Young Poet on the Underground, and in 2016 was a winner of the Poetry Business New Poets Prize. Her poems have been published in *Datableed*, *Blackbox Manifold*, *No Prizes*, and *Ambit*. She has read at the Southbank Poetry Library, Hi Zero, and with The Dead [Women] Poets Society.

Christopher
after Anthony McCall's Meeting You Halfway II

i.

Standing in the light with you is
something. At first we were
too scared to interpose our bodies
between the source and image,
but after breathing in the room,
and twanging at the minor beams
with curious hands, we took
the light onto our shoulders, backs
and faces. Disturbing the dust
that hung stilly in the air made it
a tiny sea around our waists.
If you stare into the light directly
it is like a tunnel. The heat of the beam
is like a tongue, or real sunlight.
It is December in a darkened room.

ii.

Two days after your leaving
I imagine really meeting you
halfway, somewhere in the Atlantic.
We do not fear the sea-trenches,
but sit on the bed collecting
shells and other items, pointing out
their brightnesses. This is only
another sea I want to throw myself
into. At New Year maybe,
the whole thing will just freeze over,

and we will be the first to find
each other on the ice.

iii.

Since our time in the installation,
where our bodies met the beam halfway,
everything becomes a sort of wave.
I translate whole days to light
and interruption: the sudden glow
of messages, the forms of winter strangers
crossing roads, changing the composition
of the street. *Chiaroscuro*, a word
like the flight of birds. And, finally,
our imagined bodies meeting, how we will
interrupt each other's light. Living
is a constant meeting-you-halfway,
a gradual haring down the tunnel
towards another kind of light.

iv.

It is half-midnight. Father does not see
the light that shows his daughter
slipping out the door like an old song.
She goes for the man last seen in something
like a darkroom, or *camera obscura*.
A moving with the seasons, west. Leaving
at night recalls the place she loved him
most in, the gloom that best curates the finer
points of light. This photograph. Now
I'm on my way. I'll see you in the light.
I'm meeting you halfway.

The Bat

these are not the wings
I asked for: for fewer cells

you could have made me
a bat, or bird, even a mole –

I wouldn't have to see.
just something velveteen

and small. I'm fond of pines,
and wearing black; am envious

of powered flight. when I go
to sleep I imagine bleeding

from the crooks of my arms,
of the bones breaking out

into flying apparatus. I'll be a bat,
I know, and when I am

a black rag over snow I'll be
afraid of the obscurity of water.

Flora

I think very often of our moments that night
in the fellows' garden, how time sped quickly
through our hands like rain, half-against.
On the lawn, under the dark was so much
running across the bottom of a lake, the easiness
of water, and I in my silver skirt a would-be fish,
a telling flashlight, a gift that gives away. I left
with light bruises on my legs, and a scratch
all the way from the back of my arm to
the shoulderblade. A lived-in relic, the comfort
of a body that feels itself and loves the ache
that proves potential for risk. As ever I think
of Eve clambering over the sidegate out of Eden,
her delicate skirt of leaves.

JENNY DANES

Jenny Danes was born in Chelmsford in 1995 and studied English Literature and German at Newcastle University. In 2013 and 2016 she was highly commended in the Bridport Prize for poetry and in 2016 she won The Poetry Business New Poets Prize. Her work has appeared in various magazines including *The Rialto*, *Magma*, *The North*, *Brittle Star*, and *The Kindling*. Her pamphlet *Gaps* was a winner of the New Poets Prize published with smith|doorstop in 2017.

Gaps

Everything is so divided where the sun's cut off
that it looks like someone's peeled back a strip of sky.
A daddy walks his little girl down steps and counts them
eins – zwei – drei – sehr gut. This is what she will learn.
I can't see the lake because the sun is this huge smudge
blinding it out; in fact I can't see anything except the sun
and this is what the prospect of our date feels like.
I can breathe easier out here although fuck my fingers
are really hurting and I do worry and wonder if we will kiss
or more or nothing. Last time we ate and I brushed your hand
and apologised. Now the sky is the colour of parma violets
and the dad and girl are waving at the ducks
although she won't call them ducks. What is this complete
chance that you and I were brought up in different tongues?
How is it that we would name the same object or feeling differently,
and always have done? The gaps come out in my cold breath,
between my teeth, in the groping pauses when I talk –

Shower

It's beautiful because   it's not sexual
   it's human   and clumsy   and there's love

you use my shampoo   and I wash your back
I have the gift of your form   the inches I've not seen before

the way your arm hair turns   dark and matted
   the small of your back   the gaps between your toes.

Under the water I am   trapped   and therefore
opened to you   mouth and eyes flooded

not seeing or speaking   but knowing
you're looking at my face   with such simple   boldness

at a moment when nobody's   looked at it
before.   The shower is the strangeness

of reclaiming a body as your own   after joining it with another
   of losing   the sweet animal smell
                                     of the night

Jenny Danes

Deutsch

Oh but come and chat out of the little sewing box!
How deep is the sea? I am as happy as a snow king,
I'm on cloud seven, tousled and cosy with my tootle sack –

write that behind your spoon. Blow cake, I was sure I'd be fine
but I'm standing on the hose today. Let's leave the church
in the village. A friend of me interests herself for nozzle beetles.

What goes down? A glow pear, an ice bear, away sickness,
a rain shield, a strike wood to make a flame. In the spring
should the little geese flowers and Easter bells come.

I have the nose painted full. This is a case of the spirit
splitting itself. Yes, exactly, you've met it in the black –
but also shot yourself in the knee. He's got two left hands.

Now we really are sitting in the ink. Nose horn, Nile horse,
belt animal, luck mushroom. I'm speaking in the wind.
I hope this'll conquer your heart in the storm.

Notes on missing a person

This is his body   written for me
his chin will be the last to go   I know its beard
the way a child knows texture for the first time
top of his chest, yes, but I'm a little vague
about the nipples   stomach, backside, mouth most
definitely   I've lost the legs and hands, to forget his hands
how could I   I know his neck and his freckles
I remember noticing them for the first time
This is my body   it does not know what to do
it is learning what it means to be untouched
it is singing from the rocks   it has no trust in memory
and does not believe he was ever here   it is retreating
to belong only to itself   it is ordinary again
it cannot understand   the lack of him

JEI DEGENHARDT

Jei Degenhardt was born in Manchester and studies at the University of Cambridge. Poems have been published in *PN Review*, *Stirred Press*, *Notes*, *From the Lighthouse*, and on the Young Poets Network. Jei is a prizewinner of the Midland Future Manchester Competition and the Portico Poetry Prize.

Sonnet – house party

     Lingering now for a house party – *You're all staying*, delights the Host. Falls
of ash banished through sliding doors.
 One mattress piled with rocks.
 No big deal, even if Abel swan nests
into decks and bets, drinking dealing games,
amidst courtiers, supplicants, hopeless hopefuls.
He's the lap where hopes curl to die.
    So soon.
   Desires aborted. Cheering: – *Beyond all league!*
Now twirling the Queen of Hearts to crimson.
 – *Regicide!* Happy just to lie. Smiles all over.
Abrupt undoings. New rounds of forfeits. Longings
born at a glance. Gone. Everyone joins this game.

Glaukós

The night I am in close trapping air
out of rooms and *the moon* on black windows
and pavements but gone by clouds and angled roofs
walls holding all this scent of storm the waters reach to
so low beneath the city keeps by buildings preserving
the breath the smog and *no big deal, it's a culvert,*
the walled in river coated concrete the Shibuya,
and the Seine breaking itself again in a stretch joints
popping it turns in its sleep, I'm landlocked in Still –
water okay feeling for once and the *I want*
to die and the *calm* that isn't there and a place
dammed by inorganic municipal naming but our legs dangle
over the water and when they're loose the soles of
our shoes tugging away longing *downstream*, dowsing,
the Cam doesn't even mean much to me by the tourists
the poem the eddies lost rhymes floating off spotted sometimes
along with the rhythm of the surface electric none of it meaning a thing
– except when it's green.
along with the gone, *the old man sleeping*
by the boat houses where the boats sleep the Bridge of Sighs,
with the name it dredged,
I need the Sunswick Creek while it's in exile the River Fleet I need the Rio Hamza
underground too beneath the Amazon though that can't be its real name
it is names and names of being I need the subterranean chamber of black
sand and salamanders (I need the place where Juturna turned hid
herself in a blue-green veil *and plunged, moaning,*)
somewhere in Italy, wasn't it?
where life bled down from the mountains

last month I was in crowds surrounded by strangers thinking
I knew them, this month I am seeing your face where it
isn't, thinking *doesn't guilt feel this way?*

Jei Degenhardt

KYM DEYN

Kym is a university student and part-time fortune teller living in the North East. She enjoys reading the works of Sappho, T S Eliot, and Sean Borodale.

Dog Violets

I didn't fit the fish crates set out for me

so all their whispers turned to
wives' tales, and the sound
was the sound that the sea made,
when waiting for the fishermen
to come home,

and yet, if I grew flowers from
my collar bones, if I was
a golem, all clay and dog violets
and I laid in the moors and my
curves became a valley

they would not see me the same

LOUISE ESSEX

Louise Essex is 22. She is currently studying for a Masters at UCL in English Literature, having done an undergraduate degree in English at the University of York, where she joined The Writing Squad. She runs the poetry blog @Poetry_Jar and reviews for the Poetry Book Society whilst living in London.

Half head

I only want your half head
your plaster white moon chin
in line
with my sleepy eyes

just a space
warm and hollow peachness
so helpful
for a face

eyeless and speedless
not those black pupils
that flicker to jewels
not to weave pattern
into your stringy lips
with my clammy morning mind

I want this space for me

an arm to collar my throat too
so these squeaky eyes won't
dart or dilate

All that I desire is balloon-headed.

Cancer

In your bath you were naked,
bald, purplish and slippery.

It had been so long, I couldn't get you out.
The tub was so big; you were so thin.

A soaked spine flopping there,
breastless and acquatic.

Why did your
maggot lips smile up at me
when I brought you a towel?

As if I could rub you down and find skin.
As if you could feel dry.
As if your bath would ever end.

Oysters

I feel older in the evening,
here with you.
Lunches, lunches make me feel like a child.
But here
sitting across the table from you
in amber
bulb lighting
and my bubbling throat
and us
laughing on the night

Louise Essex

SARAH FLETCHER

Sarah Fletcher is an American-British poet currently living in London. Her poetry has been published in *The Rialto*, *The London Magazine*, and the *Morning Star*. She has been a Foyle Young Poet of the Year and a two-time recipient of the Christopher Tower Poetry Prize. Her first pamphlet, *Kissing Angles*, was published by Dead Ink Books in 2015 and was shortlisted for a Saboteur Award. Sarah is a winner of the New Poets Prize 2016/17.

Wives and Girlfriends

I like how he says she is nothing   and does not mean her body
but I think of her body   It tucks into itself like a rotting peach

Anorexia is about virginity
                    I wonder whether this means I can ask you
to get your first marriage annulled   It's why my friend told me
bulimics are always promiscuous   and the joke's on them
it doesn't even work   It's all about what you let into yourself
                                    and what you don't

Wives don't want to take up space   Neither do girlfriends
I wonder if it upsets them how much space they take up in my head
like his tongue in my mouth   his fingers in my mouth
I am nobody's girlfriend   I am nobody's wife

I want him to love me until my skin is the bristled purple
of a skinned ferret   the same colour as the inside of my mouth
when I die   I will force him to look at it all on the hospital bed
so the image circles in his mind   every time he fucks someone new

I ask him how he'd murder me if he had to   and when he says he wouldn't
I say   if you were forced   and make him get real graphic
especially about   how and where   would he dispose of my body

I want him to say my name like it's written in cursive   I want his wife
to never wear white again
    I want to say I do   I do   I do

Christina Crashes The Wedding

She is invited because she'd be noticed more by her absence   than her presence
and her absence would be seen   as my own moral weakness   by the other guests
I see her at the reception   mouthing ABBA   to my husband   SOS   Her smile
the equivalent of   of a conspiratorial hand-squeeze   The way she flirts   ça va?
sounds like she's calling out my name   but the Ministry told me these
mishearings   are to be expected   from a bride of my unusually young age

I recognise the curl of her nails   the coiffed eyelashes for her fingers   from the times
she's held my mouth open to pour Malbec down my throat   tonight it's the nice stuff
imported pinot noir   and most of it gets on my milk-web dress   and the   groom says
darling you should have really worn a bra   *it's winter*   the stiff tips of my nipples
give   the wrong signal   that somehow I enjoy this   somehow   this is what I wanted
and   uh oh sweet wife the Ministry is sorry to report   there are Christinas everywhere
          you better hide the groom

The Occupant

He stayed in our flat for three months.
His body was a terrible anchor and the lichen
he brought with him soiled our couch:
the grey polyester wet, barnacled, and barely livable.
His voice was a museum of aristocracy.
The sad violin of his breathing shuttered us awake at night.

Still, we went on as normal.
We cooked him dinner, and ignored the tobacco
molting from his skin. Ignored the indents
on the couch when he moved: so deep
we could store bottles in their scope. We learned to love him.
First, almost as a pet, and then, as the landscape
in which our lives unfolded indelicately as
origami swans undressing into their original paper square.

One day, he just got up and left. Something about a girl.
Something, blonde. Something, pint in North London.
My husband and I orbited around each other for a week,
fixing a third drink each night in case he came back, still.
On the seventh night, my husband pulled a whiskey bottle
from the trench of a cushion. Then, two glasses. Ice. Soda.
We really have to do something about the couch, he said,
and I nodded. But we didn't move, and it did not fix.

Fragments/Campari

His skin went patchwork red from smoke.
They walked from the flat to the train platform.
The sun was bright and exposed all the dirty corners of their faces.
He tried to kiss her regardless, but her lips wilted and did not want to be kissed.
She walked downstairs from the bed which was not hers
to hear them talking about revolutionary Greece.
Smoke molted from their lips. It was almost morning.

In the bed, she couldn't feel her nose or her teeth, which worried her.
She was not worried about what was happening downstairs,
placing faith in his conscience and in his impotence. Downstairs,
he was kissing another woman to music from a childhood younger than his.
The woman he was kissing knew the lyrics and he did not.
This should have worried him, but it did not.

Earlier, they were drinking together, the three of them. He poured
the women Campari and the stream of the red liqueur was glamorous
as the slim neck of an outstretched flamingo, preening itself
in the Savannah sun. The sun was setting and reflected on the lake
like something spectacular and cinematic, and it was red, like Campari.

Sarah Fletcher

ELIZABETH GIBSON

Elizabeth Gibson is a Masters student at the University of Manchester and a Digital Reporter for Manchester Literature Festival. She is a member of Squad 8 and her work has appeared in *The Cadaverine, London Journal of Fiction, Now Then, Far Off Places, Octavius, Severine, Myths of the Near Future* and *Ink, Sweat and Tears*. She tweets at @Grizonne and blogs at elizabethgibsonwriter.blogspot.co.uk

Old rain

The girls who bullied me at school
work in shops and salons, show off
their hairstyles on Facebook, pose
for photos in club bathrooms on a
Friday night. They will marry local
boys and stay put, send their kids
off to our school to torment mine

– except I am gone, I am sitting on
a sandy shore, speaking in tongues
that fizzle and smoke, savouring a
passion they will not think to taste.
I wear no make-up, shove my hair
into a messy tail and stand, walk
the streets under a purple sky that

twitches with heat and stars. Have
I won? If only it were that simple.
My home town is my blood and
its wind grabbed my hair and its
rain lashed my lips and my throat
knew its snow before any foreign
fruit. I cannot outrun it so easily.

Eden

Beside the old Nile Apep handled the chaos
and now eons later the world is in slumbers
as dreaming we dive for those magical numbers
to bring back those halcyon days of Emmaus.
You are among it, a corked bottle bobbing,
dirty black water dares not touch your hair.
It sees you are broken, and hungry and bare
but under your white sheet of flesh it hears throbbing
the heart of a bat or a bumbly bee purring
dancing in blindness towards something sugared
knowing quite fully that we are all buggered
but knowing as well that the mayflies are stirring
to live their one day on this land bled and rugged.
You choke through the oil, your Eden their whirring.

Elizabeth Gibson

Going

There is a dead mole outside my
window, all fat grey belly and
little spade feet. I didn't know how
small one could be. A baby? Don't
know. He is like an oval bead, and
for all I knew about moleskin being
soft I never really got it until now.
He is the silkiest thing I have ever
seen. I just can't stop *looking* at him.
The first flies are coming and soon
more will flock around and he will

start to go. I could bury him but
the grassy heaps of land tucked into
my building are treacherous. I don't
want to see a mole rot. But I guess
he has to go back to the earth and
become nutrients, energy; make
something new. A breeze caresses
the tall stems. The noise they make
is loud, the movement quiet. I feel a
breath out. I feel something leaving.

JAMES GIDDINGS

James Giddings is a poet and curator of his own biography. Traditionally this is the place in the biography where he exaggerates his success. Here is where he lists his extensive experience of editing to add a whiff of wisdom. At the end though is where he tells you his book *Everything is Scripted* has been published, but don't fall for it, it's a ploy to get you to buy it. You're better than that.

Popsicle

The father inside my freezer shivers
clutching a bag of frozen peas
like the pillow of a son who's recently passed
to something unfortunate. All day
the motor of the freezer, its earnest whirring.
Not knowing what to do, he moves on
to the baby carrots, swaddles them
and coos. There are choices to be made.
His legs are an inconvenience the way
they're folded next to the pizza boxes.
I pile things on top of him how an undertaker
might shovel dirt on the dead
to cover the shame of dying. I bury him
under sprouts and unbranded vanilla
ice cream, so he might never be dug out
until the holidays. All this time alone
and cold, never offering to fill the ice trays.
Each day he is a paler blue. A blue
that struggles to prove how devastating it is.
How dark this room is with the lights off.
How seldom each visit. But when I reach
for some old meat bagged up as leftovers
there is a tugging at my sleeve,
and I am reminded of the father inside
the freezer, still holding on to the sunrise
of the swinging cellar light, which is constant
and warm as the love of a good son.

Instead of You Here

In your absence I have had to make do with the simplest
of dads: a wooden spoon pulled from its home
among the whisks and the loose-nutted pizza cutter.

The face I drew on the convex side is smiling.
Maybe it's wrong of me to assume your happiness
Spoon-dad, but I hope you'll be proud of me.

The pumpkin soup I make is delicious, you say,
and then roll your head in it. That's the kind of support
I've always dreamt of. You are much deeper

than my real father: the bowl at the back of your head
could hold me forever, my body a precious egg
to be carried through the course of your life.

You'd never forget how I loved you unconditionally,
the way teaspoons often mix with dessert spoons
and find a home, a family. Maybe he has a spoon

son, my other father, or a set of spoon children.
How polished he'd keep them, with their own special places
laid out beautifully around the breakfast table.

In another life

I died. It was that simple.
In another life separate to that life I was a scarecrow getting my straw-guts pecked out by the birds.
In another life I took a life … to the movies because that life was beautiful in the dress it wore and had brushed its teeth before the kiss.
In another life I lived a life inside a life, and how terrible that, that someone should have to live so much in so short a time, so complicatedly.
In another life I coughed and a lung fell out.
In another life something happened to the water and I woke up the next day not remembering anything to do with my lives before it.
In another life I stopped believing in reincarnation; how stupid that life was.
In another life I lost three fingers and twelve toes, but it didn't feel like a
                                      great loss.
In another life I thought this would be it for me, but I was proved wrong with this life, and that's made the difference.

SARAH GONNET

Sarah is a writer and autodidact from the North-East of England. She makes work in a variety of forms. Her poetry book *Voices* came out in 2016 with Survivors Press. In 2017 she received a grant from DadaFest to develop a novel based on the life of Louise Bourgeois. She is the editor of *The Female Gaze* film magazine, and is currently under commission by Random Acts to make a short film about the beautiful structures to be found in the homes of compulsive hoarders.

Psychosomatic

A word that eats itself.
Ice cubes press hard,
up from in my stomach.
My leg has an ache in
the veins like a
tree pattern all down
the bridge of bone.
Blue stones in my eyes,
swell out like sleep,
but in pebbles. Growing,
sticking, falling out
of my eyelashes.

The Girl Who Lived in a House Made of Books

The girl who lives in the house made of books
has never smelt a rose;
but she can describe their scent.
The girl who lived in the house made of books never
knew what time it is. She didn't know
where her house lay
in relation to the houses of other girls.
The girl grew up in the house made of books; sprouted roots
into their pages and fed on their energy.

Her branches grew bright green fingers. Her face became tough.
The girl absorbed words easily
because she knew she would never have to say any.
For all the effort her nimble hands
made towards the book chimney,
out into the risk of sky above,
they could never make it.
One day they stopped trying.

Another day an outside force shut off the lights in the house of books.
The girl could no longer read. At first she shouted
"I'M NOT HUNGRY ANYWAY."
But by day four of darkness she was withering.

By day eight the girl's roots came loose,
she found herself falling forever.
She tried to grip the wall with her green hands,
but soon ripped open.

By day twelve the girl was flaking away.
She lay on the floor. Her hands were brown and crisp,
yet the juice vessels were bloated with toxins.
Someone had put poison
in the darkness she was forced to breathe in.

Sarah Gonnet

On day sixteen the girl who lived in the house made of books set herself on fire.
The girl was overjoyed
that she could read again in the light of the fire.
She laughed in the face of the flames;
at her inky reunion with the letters.
She was so distracted that she didn't notice
when the house itself caught alight.

She screamed as the house turned to ashes.
The house was gone.
The house was dead.
The house was powerless.

The girl reached out with her hopeless dried veins
and creased her thick-skinned face towards the great blue risk.
She still couldn't reach where she wanted to be.

On day twenty the girl who lived in the house made of books robbed a library.
She began building her next house.

JESSICA HANSON

Jessica Hanson is a 19 year old poet and psychology student who enjoys reading, travelling and baking. She is particularly inspired by nature and European sculptures.

Possibly

You might have seen me, walking,
out of the corner of your eye,
while you were on a bus.

And for a split second your heart might have leapt:
you might have thought I was that person
but then my hand would move in an unfamiliar way,
you would realise I was, in fact,
a stranger.

So our parallel lives would continue.

All I would be was someone
who could have meant something
to you.

Enough Water To Drown
after Bob Dylan– 'Lily, Rosemary And The Jack Of Hearts' (1975)

She fills the bath with just enough water.
Not enough to drown in, she thinks.
And she should know, she does know, how much water is too much water.
Enough to drown in.
Rosemary sighs. She bathes quickly and sparingly.
That was how she lived now, quickly and sparingly.
She stands naked for a moment in the bathroom and looks at her body.
Only for a moment though, she can only bear a moment.
She turns her head away and pulls on her dress.
It doesn't matter though.
No one will come and visit her, she knows that.
She could be naked all day if she felt like it.
She never would, though, she has had enough of being naked,
she has been naked all her life and now she prefers to hide her body,
keep it under wraps so that the possession of it remains solely hers.
It had belonged to someone else for too long.
Rosemary lies on her bed and stares at the ceiling.
She closes her eyes and tries to sleep.
What is the point, she thinks, of sleeping, now?
I know I will not, I know I *can* not.
And so she lets her thoughts drift and as they drift they wander on to Lily, oh Lily.
Rosemary smiles. She lets them wander.

LIZZI HAWKINS

Lizzi Hawkins is a poet from West Yorkshire. She shares her time between her hometown of Leeds, and Cambridge, where she is reading for a degree in Engineering at Corpus Christi College. She has been commended as a Foyle Young Poet, and her work has appeared in magazines including *The Rialto*, *The Cadaverine* and *The Compass* magazine. She is a winner of the 2016/2017 New Poets Prize.

Kissing the geographer

was best. His mouth folded up
like two ox-bow lakes put together.
He touched my neck and said
it was the white of a coastal stack.

The geographer would comb my hair out
and wade in it like water –
he had hands that had known riverbeds,
the innards of a seismometer trace.

On weekends, the geographer liked to go out
into the country with a compass
and the latest OS. He would say:

I'm just old school like that, baby

and flip his hair like a horse.
I'd turn off my phone GPS to make
the experience more enjoyable for him.

He'd unfold the map on his bonnet,
circle landmarks with a biro,
trace the local river back through its tributaries,
often hold my hips, find the source in my mouth.

Train poem

The crows are lifting off like black film, peeling.
I haven't spoken to you in person for four days now.

The train goes past a yard of sheet metal
and a postage plant and I can't work out

if I'm emptying out or filling back up
with all of these cities at the same time

it's all of these cities and the lack of stopping
Manchester is a spreading pool in the distance.

It is really a corkscrew in my chest now
I miss my home and my other home.

Bradford did you miss me you're a steely husband
with filter paper in your teeth.

Bradford did you miss me no wait don't answer the question.
When I came home yesterday I was almost shaking

and the sensation hasn't yet gone.
I took a bath and the storm grabbed the window

almost off its hinges.
The wind is a warning I can't stop thinking isn't a warning.

I can't stop thinking about a boy with fat white fingers
and a house on Lensfield Road.

It's that feeling that you've been tapped like a tree
and it's all coming out.

If I were an oak tree I'd have green under my fingernails
and schoolgirls would light up underneath me on rainy afternoons.

When we went over the canal I wondered about locks
how many men it took to lift the water over the Pennines,

all that weight on their backs.
This cold country is ungrateful for our labours,

we should take off somewhere else and be trees together.
I haven't been home in a while now and I think it would be nice

I haven't been home in a while now I miss
my bedsheets, the way light pools

behind my curtains as if it is waiting to touch me.
I know you've been waiting to touch me

but I've been ignoring your phone calls and text messages.
I've been waiting to touch someone else I don't know if you're aware.

There's four hours of safe distance between us
that's not enough that's far far too much.

I should like to peel myself out of all of this like a bird
and go back to my parents' house.

Lizzi Hawkins

Winter poem

The fens were frozen clean over this morning,
from the millpond out to the causeway,
where cars flow past in a way that is not unlike sleep.

I woke up at 4am, went outside and touched the frost

– you'd left the window open and I couldn't help but leave,
scrunch my toes down into the grass, observe

the gradient of the fog on the lawn, how it was almost blue.
I should have woken you, told you how close we were to snow,
that it should've rained in the night, that we could have

had that white blessing roll itself across the fields,

tug its pale hem over the city, blunting the spires,
allowing us a brief peace.

Snow is a gift – a cold measure to be held
between the tongue and the roof of your mouth
when breathing, or to be rolled up into ice

and held on the palm. We could do with a gift
right now, could do with being bundled up and held
by the whiteness, could do with our voices

being taken away, so that we cannot say these
hurtful things any longer.

KATHERINE HENDERSON

Katherine Henderson is a poet and blogger based in Edinburgh. Her blog, pinupsandpanicattacks.wordpress.com, looks at vintage fashion, mental health and self-care. Her latest project is a series of drawings called #projectladybutts which celebrates all kinds of femme beauty.

Coal

Before I was possible,
there was your charcoal body,
hungry like an ember and knotted up.
Burnt, matchstick legs.
Hairline catching fire, consuming.
Eyes, hottest part of the flame.

Where there's a will, there's a way out.

Plait hanging like a rat in your hand.
Brass polish got under your nails.
Pewter dirt worked its way out
of your skin.
Scrubbed clean. Dried between your toes.
The coal dust on your books' spines
never came out.

Amber

under fierce sunlight
I've grown a little
apple tree in my entrails
I plant guts in the bare earth
placenta – 9 months' fertiliser

under copper veins
and dirt muscles
my bones are amber
a form born of metals
and semi-precious things

Daily devotion

Lay your foundation –
Use hands, brush or blender
to cover all over.
Smooth out from centre.
Conceal everything out of place or uneven.
Shed light on dark circles.
Put away blemishes for later.
Pinch your cheeks and set with powder.
Sculpt brows into archways
where men will try and find you.
Prime and pigment eyelids –
bright, matte white
is a quick-fix face-lift.
A jet black spine down the lash line
ends in wings.
Dress lashes in black for lift.

Always end with the lips.
Start where you sulk –
scalpel sharp tip draws blood
red outline.
Stay in the lines.
Blot twice and draw your finger
through your lips –
Get rid of excess.

KATHERINE HORREX

Katherine Horrex works as a potter. Her poems have featured in the *Times Literary Supplement*, *PN Review*, *Morning Star*, and others, and are due in an animal themed anthology from The Emma Press.

Polycystic

Ultrasound shows them:
moth holes
in the vacuum of the ovum.

Medics refer to 'strings of pearls',
some of which teethe,
their tissue is that much an assortment of cells,

casting out hair and bone to become
small sacks of offerings stored
in the tract.

Cyst hairs,
even without the scan wand
painting this wall before children,
the idea of them is clear,
grounding me like pebbles.

I leave the hospital for home
where I don't keep
plants in urns, their roots all stoppered
with gravel.

I will try to induce myself,
conducting the passage of a lunar month
through measures of darkness and light.

I am waiting for my body to snow.

Parliament, Fallen
after Park Hill Flats, Sheffield

We can afford to know nothing
beyond its concrete, the concatenate
glower of windows.
The street below is a shortcut
for us, though we hate being dripped on
by clothes horse balconies.

Looking up means a view
through a dark kaleidoscope,
where leaden basslines beat
at the air with all the thunder of hives.
It calls to mind the shuttered
instability of hearts.

As a disused mall this polygon
could be acceptable.   Instead
we wonder if there are people
in the hidden parts of the panopticon,
waiting to reveal just how
brittle they've become.

We find a helter-skelter's
skeleton bleach-stripped by the sun,
the sweet vomit smell of bleach itself,
and we consider
whether something built purely to function
can only fall to ruin,

the city's sirens congregating
in these quads,
where anyone talking talks boldly
in a voice that spreads to fill the space
shaped to keep its own
community of echoes.

LYDIA HOUNAT

Lydia Hounat is a British-Algerian poet from Manchester, England. She has been published with *Vanilla Sex Magazine*, *Hobart*, and *The Cadaverine*, as well as other publications. A photographer and performance poet also, she has had her photos published in *Peach Magazine*, and showcased her work at the Manchester Literature Festival. She is completing her English degree at Falmouth University in Cornwall, and runs a blog called LYMHPOETRY, featuring poetry based on adolescent experiences written by a fictitious alter-ego called LYMH. She is also a poetry editor for *REALITY BEACH* magazine. You can find more of her work at her website, www.lydiahounat.co.uk

Some Of Us Do Not Have Freckles

I scrub my feet in grandma's bathtub
there is a wedding outside
              oyeyeyeyeyeyeyeye
my black cousin in the playground
comes to me,
some of us do not have freckles

her smile twitches
I am ivory, like the tusk, I am no good
she can see a heavy whiteness to my cheeks
I must scrub this colour off me
I must boil the water in my lungs today

I am scrubbing the dirt out of my throat
my teeth are mud
              look at me all wasted
look at me chewing on my prayer mat
      look at them laughing at me

they call it dark humour
as black as my face
    look at me laughing
I do love stand-up comedy
now scrub this colour off me.

this is what it feels like

you wear clouds inside out
    and the rain is a crystal
it falls
it melts
into the concrete

    you're trying to drop again
the librarian is cleaning up next to you
   she looks like a she-wolf
and there are cameras everywhere

wear the sun black
  and the moon green
    you could give the night an STD
use foul language
tell him
you're a waste of time

your fingers hurt
    your back is sore
you've been crying all day
   and smiling at the kids on the news
   half-eaten by a bomb

  you are welcome
 to another piece of sky
 you are welcome to forge it
eat it,
  die in it.

Lydia Hounat

SIAN HUGHES

Sian Hughes grew up in the High Peak countryside, surrounded by hills and stone. Since moving away from this environment she has also worked on the Scottish coast, in the Highlands and Islands. Northernness, fantasy fiction, mythology and folklore started to consume her and she began writing two novels. Her poetry comes from the same place; observations about the natural world, language fits into landscape like water does. She feels connected to the land, the stories about it, our past and shared heritage. Now that she is in London, her homeland, landscapes and languages are singing back to her like sirens – tempting her back to the rocks.

Gannet

White flash against the
backdropped land,
you plunge out of the epic grey
a plot point, a forward slash,
seen for miles your wake
must rustle as you dash to make
your kill. Hunger plagues your
enraptured audiences as they
think of juicy prizes.
Pencil-tip wing-points
you make the point gracefully
that colloquially you've been
misrepresented.
It's easy to think of you as greedy
but not so, just quick, just enough
the sea sates your urges, thrift
and food and acrobatics.

HANA KAPETANOVIC

Hana has been writing pretty much her whole life, from terrible stories to slightly better stories to poetry to journalistic articles. When she isn't writing in English, she's attempting to string sentences together in Arabic and hopes to one day be able to write Arabic poetry. She has been published in her university newspaper and magazines, in online 'zines, and various anthologies and is constantly developing her writing style and interests.

A Scenic Moment

It is hard to have a scenic moment on a park bench
when we are trying to forget what our thighs look like,
spreading shamelessly across the wooden surface,
as if entitled to that space. We allow them a moment of peace
before we remember to hover, uncomfortably, to be smaller,
more natural.

It is scenic, this moment. Birds chirping, green overflowing
its allotted space on the banks, like the soft rolls over our jeans.
It is okay not to breathe when someone walks past
if we allow ourselves to exhale afterwards, cursing
the elderly woman and her tiny steps, marvelling
at her tiny wrists. We hold our breath harder,
more natural.

Scenically, simultaneously, we hold pastry which we bite
at intervals, pretending not to time the seconds in between.
One, two, bite. Three, four, bite. Five, six, bite.
We must look like goddesses, feeding ourselves grapes,
hair flowing down our backs. But we are down-to-earth –
not thin enough to float into space. Beautiful
but approachable – we sometimes digest calories too,
natural – like the girls in the photos,
scenic, if someone were to walk past.

How To: Romance

You were the kind of nice you see in the cinema:
pulling out chairs, paying for dinners, walking the girl home.
The kind that reads the rose petal, candlelit dinner
guidebook for romance but falters at the execution.
You pulled out chairs, sometimes, wined and dined, once,
under the golden arches of McDonalds, saying
you would have walked me home if it weren't for the rain.
You were several thousand rain droplets from romance
and stopped short of buying me flowers – they grow
too much, too wild, too unpredictable,
and gardening was never your strong suit.

The continuity of substance

How do you know if they're the one?
She talks about that new album with casual precision
in a language you're not quite familiar with
and cannot replicate, at least in this universe.
You hear the inflections of her voice and realise
you like music, too. The album, anything.
She talks about it as a matter of urgency;
you must listen. Every fibre in your body complies
whether your mind likes it or not. You'll listen tonight
when you have undressed and prepared yourself
not to be seen until morning. You will find the song,
smiling about a joke someone made at dinner, and listen.
Sometimes when we listen we do not hear ourselves.

How do you know if they're the one?
You like it when they lean in closer, savouring
every last syllable. There is something about you
that they seem to enjoy, and so you keep going.
You are rewarded with laughter you have heard before,
laughter echoing in restaurants with small tables.
Two former strangers leaning in, taking turns.
People are funny when others laugh, which feels like
a bridge between brains full of chaotic thoughts.
If a joke falls in a forest and nobody is there to hear it,
is anyone ever really funny? After a while,
you can no longer tell what you're laughing about.
Sometimes we feel as flimsy as bridges.

How do you know if they're the one?
You just know, apparently. Hume rolls over in his grave.
You know until you don't. It feels right until it doesn't.
You look at him for the thousandth time and this time
you cannot stand his laugh. You wonder how you ever could.
Where were you this whole time? Leafing through old
conversations is alien, like looking back at childhood photos,
asking yourself how it is that you are that same person.
It might be that you are not. You have hair now,

although your judgement is still shaky, mistaking
rumbles for butterflies. Perhaps you want to.
Can you want yourself into otherness?
Sometimes all you know is that you don't.

GREGORY KEARNS

Gregory Kearns is a poet based in Liverpool. He has been published in magazines such as *The Lifejacket Anthology* and *Independent Variable*. He has also written for performance with Tmesis Theatre Graduate company in 2016 and on The Wonderous Stories artistic residency in Ommen Netherlands in 2015. He is particularly inspired by the works of Wislawa Szymborska and Paolo Sorrentino.

Pneumatophore

I stand, thigh deep in hurricane water, murky from home foundations
                                                          churned into soup.
My legs brush against orange traffic cones. I feel no sensation of wetness.
I am there to make a documentary, to capture sound and footage.

I wade in the wake of the guide

He points to the shifting landmarks that signpost the way,

though tomorrow it could signpost something else. He takes us to a
                                               sacred place,
one that doesn't move. We are there at dusk and I feel my chest constrict.

One mangrove tree clings to this waterscape. Supple roots jutting
                                               from the water,
anchoring the tree.

This mangrove, Guardian of the Coast, could protect nothing.
This mangrove, a desperate claw, holding few lives.

Hooked: a rucksack, a necklace, an empty dog collar.

This mangrove is crippled.

I turn to the crew to see if they are capturing it. Just outside of its roots,
a group of snakes flail together. A vigorous tangle, like earphones.
One snake stares at me. I am scared it will reach out with fangs, anoint my
neck with its symbol. Two symmetrical puncture wounds, like red tear ducts.

I wake, sitting on damp sand on a bright beach, a shallow tide pulling out.
Circled around me, orange crabs. I pick one up, it snaps at my fingers.
I see many crabs
advancing, crawling forward, their legs moving forward.
I try to stand but can't.

Spacemen
based on an installation by Isa Genzken

These spacemen lying down
could save me

and I would let them
take me in their sleeping helmets;
allow them to wrap me up
in tin foil and keep me warm

if only I would cross this line.

In the dead space between mirrors.
In this dead space between people.
Where all reflections are unequal.

Expedition
first line from Matthew Sweeney's poem 'Naked'

Take off your shoes, he said
(So I took off my shoes,)

walk into my tent as big as Alaska,
(I walked in stooping at the door)

breathe in the sweat of explorers,
(I breathed in and choked on the taste)

stop writing your memoir in your head,
(I didn't)

eat the food you brought
(I ate the food and felt sick)

and sleep until the roof falls in.
(I lay awake watching the tent top slowly crumple)

Gregory Kearns

123 Cherry Tree Lane

1.

A picture of dad pointing
to the Sold Sign on the lawn

If it was in colour
there'd have been pink blossom in the grass

His glasses sliding down his face
Nose slicked with sweat

The last boxes left on the doorstep one labelled *Mark's Clothes*
the other labelled *Useful Crap Found Under the Stairs*

2.

Uncle Lee from *overtheroad*
with his flat cap on shoveling snow

Milo jumping into the mounds on the sides of the road
Me held to my mum's hip

arms outstretched for Tabs
who looked unsure about being outside

3.

Milo jumping off a roof
onto a large stack of leaves

The blur of dad entering the frame
Milo's friends looking up to him

through a beam of light
Added in spidery biro

World's Best Stunt Man
written with the wrong hand

Gregory Kearns

SAFIA KHAN

Safia Khan is an aspiring medic who writes to stay sane. Her newfound addiction to poetry started after attending a Hive South Yorkshire Arvon writing residential at Lumb Bank. Her poems are often about the women in her family, whose stories throughout generations and across continents have been her inspiration.

Grandma's Kitchen

I watch you through a fog
of onion tears, our noses fizz with mirch,
namak, garam masala. I suggest paprika.
You wipe away my tears, hands soft as kajoor,
the trace of chilli on your fingertips
sears my eye. I can see you in red,
but you are, and will always be, lilac
like the chaadar you wear over your silver hair,
and the lavender you plant between his weeds.
You get me to taste after adding the garlic,
my eyes give away – too much mirch.
You laugh. Your silly English granddaughter
can't handle the Pakistani heat.

Umma's Room

I examine the artefacts, meticulously preserved.
One red lipstick, circa 1983, used for coating
smiling lips and silver whiskers. A thumb-misted bottle
of Chanel No.5, spoiled by age, still liquid gold.

A patch of worn carpet, stale green, moth-holed.
Photo frames, each one louder than the next.
By the window, I can hear your cackling
laughter in the garden, as you hang dreams on the washing line.

A hearing aid, but you could never hear me.
I stand in your museum, and crumple like the tissues
I used to wipe your mouth. I have no audio guide
to translate you. I never learnt Punjabi, but I understood *pyar*.

Home

When I see my house from the train,
as it shrinks away while the speed grows,
I see a magnolia tree
sprinkling petals like wedding confetti.

I see a drain balcony
onto which a girl once climbed
to think about smoking cigarettes.
I see a black gate behind black bins
leading to a garden I cannot see,
where weeds have been uprooted,
by a man with cracks in his concrete smile.

I see a door opening for people the house doesn't like,
bruised by blackcurrant in places,
by people who wander in
and throw their problems about with ease,
like coats chucked on the banister.

I see smoke from a chimney,
a grey sigh of relief,
breathed out by a kitchen
where something is burning
but will still be eaten.

I see a blinking window,
with its eyes closed, because behind them
a girl is sleeping with eyes open
as her mind races along the tracks
and never pulls into the station.

Safia Khan

STEFAN KIELBASIEWICZ

Stefan Kielbasiewicz is a poet, editor and translator living in London. He is currently doing his MA in Creative Writing Poetry at Royal Holloway. He been shortlisted for the Jane Martin Poetry Prize in 2014 and the PEN International New Voices Award in 2016; his work has been published in *Ink, Sweat and Tears*. Stefan is a winner of the New Poets Prize in 2016/17.

Five-a-day

```
          Do you remember to eat your five-a-day?

          Do you carry a garden or an orchard
                       in your head?

                 Do you sink tes dents
          dans ton       second langue
          and    déchirer words  like ice
                 qui se sépare
                                from
                                                     a glacier?
                 Does ton third język
                    have twardą    skóre
     ou an           aureole              de fuzz
     mais qui   est bursting    z szrotka
                 so    that le     jus
drybluje
down
ton
menton?
                 Do you need to sbucciare
                    twoją quatriéme lingua
                 i tagliare                    do smażenia?

                 Or is your fifth язык
                 un стебель       a root
                    который нужно bouillir
                 i spruzzare    z чуть-чуть solą?
```

        Or is there
     only   one language
that you breathe
               that nourishes
this   diversity of   tongues –
and our teeth   that become the   seeds
    of
        various

Stefan Kielbasiewicz

# of a Salesman

I.

He dies while crossing the stage
towards his apartment building.

The curtain rises.

The salesman's wife stands over him,

*"Well, you'll just have to take a rest,
you can't continue this way,"* she sighs.

II.

The salesman dies in an eight-story fall
after admiring the sea-view from his balcony.

He runs a bath to soothe his aching back.

He dies the next morning, standing
with his feet in the sea-water, his skin

calcifies into a coral statue.

Dreams settle in salt behind his ears
and on his eyelids.

His salary.

*A salesman always trades
in hope, a brighter future.*

III.

The salesman dies after a successful
triple bypass. They served him *steak au poivre*

and a glass of red wine.

His wife visits him: "You don't look
too well. Have you been eating properly?"

She leaves a plate of sliced apples,
cheese and dried dates on the pillow.

IV.

What goes through a man's mind, driving
seven hundred miles without having earned a cent?

The death of a man's mind.
The death of a living.

He sells what a salesman has to sell,
himself.

V.

At his funeral the salesman tells his family:

"Things are looking very promising, I'm closing a deal
any day now."

He is a performer, a confidence man
who must never lack confidence.

We each sprinkle a handful of soil
with pistachios.

"Your father looks young," his wife
reminds her son, "but so do I."

VI.

The salesman dies many times:
the forest ranger, the cellist, the entrepreneur,
the dreamer.

He has placed his faith in the future
while being haunted by the past.

of man's mind.
of living.

The music crashes down
and the salesman becomes

the soft pulsation of a single
cello string

that keeps us all alive.

THEOPHILUS KWEK

Theophilus Kwek is the author of four volumes of poetry, most recently *The First Five Storms* (smith|doorstop, 2017) – co-winner of the New Poets' Prize in 2016. He is also the winner of the Berfrois Poetry Prize, and came in Second in the Stephen Spender Prize for Poetry in Translation 2016. Formerly President of the Oxford University Poetry Society, he now serves as Co-Editor of *Oxford Poetry*. His writing has appeared in *The Guardian*, *The London Magazine*, and *The Asia Literary Review*, among other publications.

The First Five Storms

Beginning November 2015, when the UK Meteorological Office began to name its storms.

Abigail

We sat up late one night to watch the sky
Knowing where they slept, still, in their fury,

A den of them curled on the red-rimmed ledge
Of tomorrow's weather. As we talked, we kept

Our predictions close: how long
Before the year's, and our own winters would align,

Or the rest of our days reach in to join fingers
With the season's slow dusk, and disappear.

What came afterwards, or perhaps who,
Surprised us both. It was as if they knew

Something we didn't about earth's velocity,
The speed of spring, time's machine. Soon the first

Trains arrived at King's Cross with Berwick's rain.
It was then that we learnt to give them names.

Barney

Here we sensed the war and tremble of it,
The fallen scaffolding, the leaf-filled storm,
In land-bound Oxford a river's solvent march.
For all of what we knew as Christmas
It came unspent, and there was not a room
That did not seal itself against that tide
Of fog and rain, a rippling in the sky

Like the wake of a wake. When it was past
We looked out, and went back into the street
Where there was death, and ice, and such a calm
Of winter, road-pressed tracks, a dark bonsai
Stooped by a window of our chimneyed home.
We stood, then went in our cars to church,
And scraped our shoes, and left the dog outside.

Clodagh

We made the landing that we thought we would
Three hours late, and below the flush deck
Where drivers sat at their cards, stretched and stood
The worse for wear. You had slept through the thick
Of it, so didn't feel the sudden fall
As our hull found Dublin's sterner quay, and lodged
Shuddering against the sea's dredged wall.
Above the harbour, a glassy-dark ridge –

Horizontal, like the sea's calmed veneer –
Stood across from where a guileless city lay
Behind a crowd of windows. I had come here
To make resolutions, taste the grey
Christmas skies you loved, but found instead
Fine rain, and land underfoot; gold and myrrh.

Desmond

When you had gone up to bed, that night,
A wind came and touched a corner of the roof
Which sang, through the shingles that had come loose
And shook the nest, which had been built inside.
How late, the storm that followed close behind
Locked in all its pent determination
That even love's sentry was, briefly, then,
Asleep, her once watchful head dipped within.
She made no sound as, like a ship astern,
Her bower was rushed by the northern rain.
This morning I saw her young: unlearned,
Alive. I cannot explain, love, but I knew
How different they seemed, and how they sang
All the louder in the rain, and flew.

Eva

And after several days' lowering,
White like a dream of white, ghosting snow,
There and not there as we fled from town
One pure winter's morning. Wanting to make
The most of daylight, we set out early
And with the first glare came up to the track,
Full-bodied, the scent of January's mowing
Fresh on fallen grass: a season's dowry,

Made in our time as the meadow hankered
Under a cloth of cold. What could ever come
Of such small beginnings? Already the frost
Was melting on the path, which, unbroken,
Would put dry earth to grass, and then in time
Turn road to wood, and sky, and bark, and moss.

DOMINIC LEONARD

Dominic Leonard is an undergraduate at Christ Church, Oxford. His poetry and essays have appeared in *IRIS*, *Cherwell*, *Ash*, *The Kindling* and the *Oxford Review of Books*. He was a Foyle Young Poet in 2015 for 10 minutes, before being disqualified for being 5 hours too old.

Nightmare

this is the ugliest bed i've / ever slept in. i take black and white / photos of the dirty peeling wallpaper / i trace the nailmarks in the / wood. please take shelter and forget / your loved ones. / look at me / look away. soup is the gentlest word / i could just pick it up. i make / a note to use a rollercoaster / as a metaphor for obsession. trust me / i'm a poet. did i tell you about my recurring nightmare? i make mature and informed decisions. / plum is a word that seems / quite pleased with itself. is this laugh convincing? are you listening? / imagine how terrifying it would be for / someone to know you had been here. how terrifying / it is to show people you exist at all / how terrifying it is to imagine anything for much more than a second

To a Back, 2am

        Your back
        is a bed I pass out in

          Your back
    bristles, to furrow into flowers

              Your back
reminds me we forgot to bring aspirin

           Your back
      is the dissolved, violet hours

       Your back
as an accordion in a locked room

            Your back
        as enamel, pool drain

                Your back
        is the line's soft place

          Your back
is the smell of tarmac after rain

      Your back
turns out the skin's alphabet

           Your back
     is the altar and the event

               Your back
is what it feels like to forget

          Your back
is interrupted by your hair's caught moment

Your back
makes me wish that I'd tried

Your back

does to me

what New York

does to the sky

THEODORA OYANI

Theodora Oyani is a former student of Prior Pursglove College (2014-2016). Currently she's on a gap year and working part-time. She loves to read, cook and crochet. Theodora is a member of Writing Squad 8.

Dawn

It was a brutal blue morning, not a soul
stirring awake. The birds were singing of
dawn and the night was turning to day.
Outside a grey, dull stretch of concrete, in
an emptiness closing in on itself, the stench
of poverty cloying every little space.
Two small women and a man stood,
chanting prayers, with their heads echoing
the amen.

No one was listening, everyone slept. Their
shadows, distraught, weakened, tattooed the
walls and the floors. Invisible but felt. The
woman, the older unknotted a cut of cloth,
stretched it forth with tired hands. The man,
honourable, cast it back. It was not anger,
only love. They all hugged; a symbolic
exchange from kin to kin.

Perhaps if they could grasp each other tighter
fate would let them have this moment forever.
The man withdrew, bag in hand. Walked away
and towards the gate, the red rusty one aged
with returnings and arrivals. He cast the two
small women one last glance and was gone.
The two small women, they stared ahead, their
hearts were breaking yet hope was there.

They shared a look, they tried to smile. The older
gasped, her shoulders shook. Like a worn brown
machine heaving to life. The younger reached out,
drew the older close. Comfort came then; small and
undignified. Night was still turning to day and the birds
were watching them hope.

LAURA POTTS

Laura is a Yorkshire-based poet and currently an English Literature student at the University of York. She has twice been named as a London Foyle Young Poet of the Year and Young Writer, and in 2014 became a Lieder Poet at the University of Leeds. She now collaborates with a composer from the Royal Welsh Conservatoire and in her spare time edits for York's *Looking Glass Anthology*.

Ancestors

From the sour breath of quarry towns we came,
to our scars the firelight a mother. In another land
our broken chord stretched far on the moors,
the flint of our tongue, the tinder, the coal,
hung in their black sacks our lungs sang
to the dead dark night of the child, too young
in her grave. We wore the eyes of the damned.

Our biblical chant we took to the wars,
candled the lanterns to hopes of our home,
where Madame in her manor, high summer,
forgot. In our hallway of night, watched lights
in distant houses dream up their happiness –
all the bells of Notre Dame – and mourned
in our trench, in our filth, in our lice,

for our spouses – their corpses – when our dead
stank the ground. Hometown was lonely that year.
Here, us, we never danced down promenades,
our arms like silver chimes. Our drip was slow
through time, gritted and gnarled, no child
never aspired to living to three. We got a VC.
And still died on the slump of our knees.

And in the candle of our last hour's sleep, across
the moors and the mines, sit the ghosts
of our shanties long-crippled in time. The moon,
with his holy eye of light, still sits on his swing,
smoking his pipe. Here, at night, tell them we saw
the chasms and grey seascapes of fate, the cracks
in mankind, poverty's shadows tall on the walls,
our dark graveside flowers all dead on the day
when our bones got up and, slowly, walked away.

Don't say that our stars are forgotten today.

Don't say I am nothing at all.

Merrie City

Here in the home of smoke and smog, my hometown grey,
heirloom of mines, the steam and the fog, where evening plays
on the moorland spine to colliers' paces
and the northern wind that weathered their faces

still gnarls in the teeth of the two a.m. frost;
here where tomorrow is always lost
in the death of the streetlamps hung in their hats,
their spluttering, fizzling, last-rite laughs

like the dark psalms stammered in the vestry's dusk;
here where communion no longer tolls, where cathedral musk
is a godless ghost beneath ten dead bells,
and the cold throat belfry is an old shack shell

for the alleyway hobo in his passing breath,
and his cat which brims on the edge of death;
here where the fieldlamp's first candled flame
is its last, and the quarry's trace, a stain

over skin, casts the shadow of a grieving face,
(the memento mori of this town), this dead grey place
where the factory black is the cradle we sing to,
the sack where we sleep is the home that we cling to,

only here come here to the city's dark heart,
only here come here to the tubes in its arms,
the industrial crack, these towers of ash,
where we think of the poverty coffins we'll have.

FIELDING RONSHAUGEN

Fielding Ronshaugen is a twenty-four-year old poet, writer and primary school teacher living in Manchester. She grew up in California and the North of England, which has led her to develop a keen attention to sense of place. Fielding has been previously published in *Magma*, *Cadaverine* and *Cake*. She was shortlisted for the Magma Editor's Prize in 2014, the Christopher Tower Prize in 2011 and was a winner of the Foyle Young Poets of the Year Award in 2010. She has been part of the Writing Squad for five years.

Aeolian Processes

At the beginning of the world the moon was yawned
into existence, born from the cool condensing breath

of fast moving comets reflected on still water.
The moon fell in love with the tired sea and pulled

and pulled relentlessly until oceans shuddered into waves,
sighing. This is how your personal wind was born.

Your wind had its rebellious teenage years,
she carried the first bird aloft once it had finished

that evolving business, pushed Odysseus off course,
had a run in with your many times great grandmother

while she stood high on chalk cliffs at the storm-ridden daybreak.
With clever hands, she wove your wind into superstitious ship rope.

She sang through leaves, ruffled feathers, fell in with a hurricane.
But, on the day you came alive she was ready for you as promised,

pushing her way eagerly into your barely finished lungs
before any other air had the chance. Breath that was breathed

by any number of famous people: Eleanor Roosevelt,
Shakespeare definitely, by bears on distant tundra, sleeping dogs,

breath that ballooned the lungs of the man who didn't, by some
dumb luck, kill your then sixteen year old grandfather in the war.

Your wind loves you unconditionally, unconsciously, like
only something you do not even know is with you can.

Your wind saves your marriage twice with softened
doors and brushes hair out of your eyes and steals

bad news out of your hands before you can look.
Your wind writes you letters: roughs up the sand

from the grey beach and sends it swirling out to a
lighthouse point in low billows of reverent grit.

When you die, your wind will knock the hats off of those
who think ill of you and cause no less than three

of your unpleasant second cousins to shiver
nervously at your well attended final yard sale.

She'll remember each of the letters of your name
until they are worried away from your grave stone.

When ghosts are no longer needed and every thought of
you is done, your wind will go home to the sea, and fall asleep

drifting into absence, rolled into whales' respiratory systems
and ponderous oxygen bubbles sinking to the surface.

Sarah Good

She must have wished they were right in the end,
that the black or yellow birds were her particular friends,
that a man in a dark coat had sat at the end of her bed
and taken away her name to keep it safe,
that she could leap up and sweep the stars from the sky,
and that her heart was an atlas moth waiting
to push its way up and out of her mouth.
When then she woke and Mercy was cold and still
against her breast, she must have wished
she could drink the green out
of the wheat fields in spring and deliver
the strength of tender buds however she saw fit.
She must have wished she had foreseen the natives,
moving silently though the forest to take her away.
She must have wished she could make the girls
cry out at will, pinched and bruised by unseen hands.
She must have wished she deserved it.

Celia and Rosalind

You, whose company I cannot live out of.
You, who could light a whole room with
just the colour of your lemon-soaked hair.
You, the only person on the planet that I could
stand to be the only person on the planet with.
You, with freckles like the Pleiades, reading my mind.

If everywhere we went, we paired off like swans.
If I were the kind to spangle trees with the
paper trails of love, every leaf would be
for you because I write for myself.
If we must have weddings let them
be doubled and to forgiving brothers.

ALEXANDER SHAW

Alexander Shaw is from South Tyneside and is currently studying English and German at Jesus College, Oxford. His poetry has appeared in *The London Magazine*, *Ink Sweat & Tears* and *Butcher's Dog*. He won the Martin Starkie Prize 2015, was shortlisted for the London Magazine Poetry Prize 2016 and was highly commended in the New Poets Prize 2016/17.

Landscape without Reiver

Put in Longtown and Langholm and fill with egg
tempera. Leave out the dull spool of firth.

Put in lines drawn in the sand-fells. Leave out
bastle-houses built of logs and salt, safe-for-now
steads.
      Put in pointillist sheep and sprig of gorse,
leave out another country's national flower.

Put in farm-labourers like in Bruegel's famous
The Harvesters, leave out problem clans –
Armstrongs, and Laidlaws, and Scotts –
and their strongholds, threpe lands west
of the Esk.
      Put in vanishing lines, perspective:
disappear through a peep-hole to Scotland.

Occupation

So, I turned to lens cutting for a living.
Corrective work, in a time of short-
sightedness.
         An astigmatic time
too: few saw how Os gaped
on drawn faces – none heard them.

Precise work. Blown glass alone
kept its shape, amongst so much
hot air.
       Still, a glance up
from the cutter one afternoon
was the only point I saw
violence in focus. Show pieces
were cracking up in the heat.

All summer, tyres roared in backyards,
as they burnt: there were roars
of laughter in the streets.

I made a steady living, under
the occupation. Precise,
painstaking work –

this is to correct the record.

Alexander Shaw

How to Prepare for Bad News

First, ochre your fingertips, and take helium.
For levity. Puff out any surplus gas to flame;

scrape off residue with a two inch blade,
as if scratching the seeds from a lotus

with antler-bone. Tighten the strings
around the hollow belly of a Steinway,

ribbed ivory clinking to *Winterreise*.
Muffle the extractor fan and husk

into your receiver: *Sing to me of prikaza,
messenger.* Got all that? Now I tell you.

Alexander Shaw

JASMINE SIMMS

Jasmine Simms is a Vice Chancellor's Scholar for the Arts at Durham University. She has twice been a winner in the Northern Writers Awards, most recently being named a New North Poet in 2015. Her poems have appeared in magazines such as *Magma* and *The North*, and in anthologies such as *Hallelujah for 50ft Women* (Bloodaxe), *All That's Ever Happened* (The Poetry School) and *Something to be Said* (Tower Poetry). She is co-founder of the Dead [Women] Poets Society, and a graduate of The Writing Squad.

St Chad

Ordinary Durham Lad, hauled up
from the East Midlands to Aidens College.
An undetectable accent. A secret
library under his desk. His brother,
Cedd, also a saint, scored a hatrick
against George on the last day
of term. Chad has been our friend
ever since we started having boys
for friends. It's not been easy.
First, we couldn't get him to stop
touching himself in our bathroom.
Different definitions of sacred,
we said. Then he wouldn't stop
praying in the living room.
Then he wouldn't stop telling us
his dreams. Something changed us.
Now we keep a convent
in our student house. *Chad, we miss you.*
We who saw your elevation
outside Oswald's: the drunken angels
 singing under the Cathedral's huge
shadow, the flashing blue light
that chose you, beaming you back
to wherever boys come from.

Hitching
for Lily

First piece of advice: forget instincts.
Learn by heart the better judgements

of an anxious world, the sensible
shoes and warm clothes, the impossible

distance between countries, like doctrines.
Far safer not to speak about religion.

Become good at small talk, so small
you could disappear in it, and do not

sleep in the back seats, eyes pulled shut
as though magnetised. Like how you slept

at the back of classrooms, the judgements
rumbling beneath you like submarines.

Forget yourself. For small talk use only
the true facts remembered from Biology.

For example, that women blink more
than men. You try to catch his eyes

in the wing-mirrors. He says women
on the pill blink more than anyone.

You would put this down to sleepiness.
He would put this down to chemistry.

Second piece of advice: never disagree.
Every bad decision will keep you awake

in the next place, hitching your skirt up
in the bathroom, breathing bad words

onto mirrors. But this time you gallop
into sleep. You slide the doors of vans

like lifting the skirts of girls. You wonder
if you're dreaming when it starts to feel

like school again, the autobahn dirty
and wide as the humanities corridor,

the boys in the submarines singing.
And when your Mother tells it as the story

of the time you nearly died, you remember
it as the time you could not stop blinking.

Recurring Dream

in which I am one of those born
without an oven in their stomachs,
who shout at themselves in mirrors.

Which is to say: the men. They are
all around me, hanging about under
extractor fans. An imposter, I stand

in the white coat of my ex boyfriend
who we laughed at for taking Food Tech.
But this is a manly job, isn't it?

We wrap girls in tin foil, weigh
our hearts until they are light enough.
It's hard work. We move through tunnels

and end up in the underworld
which is an indoor place, but here
my brothers use their *outdoor voices:*

the sounds of manhood, filling
the backs of our minds
like hymn tunes. They let me in.

Heaven is a large, dark kitchen.
Fill your boots, say the men
at the table, this is all there is.

Jasmine Simms

School

I wanted Boyfriends who were good at Science.
In Physics I drew love hearts, or bent and unbent
paper clips into the shape of love hearts. Whoever
doesn't know what love is hasn't been to a Physics
lesson and dragged a toy car across a desk to test
the forces on us. I tilted my hips and said 'Gravity
is the best man, Girls, he never leaves', and rolled
myself across the carpet. First Kiss was a boy who failed
his Science GCSE and it was like being dropped into
a conical flask. Outside, life went on. Inside, I started
to believe in particles for the first time, crawled my way
back into the library, under a duvet. Physics Boy said:
'If you split an atom you find the world trembling
like a newborn.' And then I stopped holding it together.

PHOEBE STUCKES

Phoebe Stuckes studies at Goldsmiths. She has been a winner of the Foyle Young Poets award four times and is a former Barbican Young Poet. She has performed at the Southbank Centre and the Poetry Cafe, and was the Ledbury Festival young poet in residence in 2016. Her poetry has been published in *The Cadaverine*, *Ink Sweat & Tears*, *Rising* and *Ambit*. Phoebe was a winner in the New Poets Prize, Judged by Helen Mort, and her collection *Gin & Tonic* was published in 2017 by smith|doorstop.

Home

If I'm left alone
I get swamped by the urge
to cut off my hair
or dye it an unnatural colour
one-handed, in the sink.

I want to wear black
but getting dressed feels
like being stood up.
I've a date with nothing.

I am swallowing endless photos
of exes in foreign countries
or at festivals. I suffocate my heart
in pasta and cheese sauce,
leave the dishes submerged

in rock pools of soap.
If I google how to know
if you're having a breakdown
the links are all purple.
Outside, seagulls are hooting

like ambulances.
I don't trust myself enough
to open an upstairs window
to watch them wheeling around.

Crisis

I don't like church
as much as I enjoy incense and guilt.
I can get the same effect

from sticks of sandalwood
and reading articles online
about natural disasters

while I'm in my underwear
eating tortilla chips out of the bag.
I only like the kind of cults

where you can talk about your feelings
and grow neat rows of vegetables,
salad in allotments

while wearing soft fabrics.
My father told me all the prophets
were reluctant prophets.

They wanted to be left alone
with their homes and their families.
Then God came along

and shook up their lives
like a snowglobe
some of them died.

I know the Church of England
Standard Worship from beginning to end
but I could also recite Dark Side of The Moon

if anyone cared to ask me.
I think both will be lodged in my head
forever and ever. Amen.

Phoebe Stuckes

Judgement

We spent our days on the phone together
in silences and shuddering gasps. There were times
I crawled into the space between my bed and the floor
and wouldn't come out until my heartbeat slowed
from a sprint to a pace. You were lost too
but you said hey, you're the one under a bed.
Your girlfriend's underwear lined the radiators
in your flat. The night a smile tugged the corner
of your mouth like knicker elastic.
You were the only person I was not afraid
to sleep next to and it made me furious
and very frightened. I caught the scent
of your laundry powder on the street
and stayed there for minutes,
pulling you out of my heart
in handfuls, like algae from a river.
Another night you told me
to just lie there, and afterwards
that we should draw a line under it
well this is it, this is that line.

Phoebe Stuckes

SOPHIE TURNER

Sophie Turner is a 23 year old poet, blogger, teaching assistant and collage artist from Rotherham. She is a member of The Writing Squad, and inspired by the work of Margaret Atwood, Alice Walker, Tracey Herd, Kim Addonizio and Rupi Kaur.

Ursa Major

In another life they'd say she asked for it.
What did she expect? Those perfect curves,
and tits clothes couldn't conceal. She'd have been a
child star, street whore, outlaw with cigarette stars
on her arms.

Used up, emptied out. Broken in beneath
the warm buzz of budget bulbs. A lead weight branding,
burning, chewing up her cherry-soft skin.
He spits the dregs back out. The pit –
chink. She sings as she hit the sky. Shattered. Halved.
Whole.

Jupiter, Zeus, Bastard man. Sky and thunder God.
Eternal slag with lust in his eye. Callisto on his mind.
All rhinestone moons and cut glass stars. Night's blue light spills
on the nylon backdrop of his cheap thrill.

The Far Side of the Moon

Then, hollows and jutting out bits –
bruised knees, bitten lips, up till dawn watching
paper chain people living unlived lives. Photographing
street lights, love bites, full-mooned nights

skies burnt out orange with sun-cloud
glows. Egg yolk yellow, and swelling from its skin.
At five, six, even seven; sleep. Seeping from my own
skin, all those broken bits and bits mulched on. Unme
verbs. Smushed up soap. Blutack. White tack.
Plasticine girl.

ELOISE UNERMAN

Eloise Unerman is based in South Yorkshire and writes poetry and short stories. She has been published in the anthology *Everyday Hymn* (Writing Yorkshire, 2015) and the *Anthology of Young Poets* (Paper Swans Press, 2017). She won first prize in the young people's category of the Hear My Voice poetry competition, as well as a commendation in Photofictions 2014, and has been awarded the Cuckoo Young Writers Award 2017.

I Saw Myself

I catch you in the post office,
mailing a package to an address
that no longer exists, licking the stamp
and screwing up your nose.
Your fingers press into poorly-wrapped
paper like a man touching hospital
sheets after waking up to realise
he doesn't know who the president
of the United States is.

I see you through the boutique window,
holding roses against your lapel,
pins between your teeth, watching
your mother flitter around you
with guest lists and invites, plying you
with wedding cake toppers, suggesting
photographers who can capture every moment
except the ones you've already lost.

You walk up the church steps, jilted
by your memories, the only knot they've tied
is the one in your stomach. You loosen
your tie and sit on a step next to a delicate line
of crocuses flattened halfway in by a boot print.
You remember then how you looked down
at your own boots when they pulled the bullet out.

Bells chime and you wonder if all you'll ever know
is that you were engaged to be married
and you hate the taste of glue on envelopes.

Glass

I used to be part of a team
a couple bought as a half-assed
gift to congratulate another
on their union. I've seen Bordeaux,

Rioja, Merlot, Champagne, but
nothing can ease the pain of watching
couldn't care less hands
smash my partner in glass.

All my problems stem
from the stubbled man
who fills me up
to knock me back.

Eloise Unerman

CHARLOTTE WETTON

Charlotte is a page and performance poet, based in West Yorkshire. She has a spoken word album *Body Politic* and has just published her first pamphlet *I Refuse to Turn into a Hat-Stand* with Calder Valley Poetry. 'Home Safe' won the Poetry Business Yorkshire prize in 2016, judged by Helen Mort. Her hobbies include fell-running and hearing about other people's careers. @CharPoetry

In Mexico

everything will be different.
We will have a house on the edge of the desert,
a yard of hot dust, a rangey dog on a chain.
Lizards will climb in the walls and one eagle
will turn and slowly turn in the blue expanse.
We will eat 'till we are full and the meat juice
runs down our chins. I'll put on a little weight
from fat-fried beans and corn and it'll suit me,
my hips tilt a little wider. In Mexico,
you will bring me flowers for my hair,
as I pour milk into a yellow bowl.
The heat will harden me. I'll wear boots with spurs,
an icon of the Virgin,
ride pillion on your motorbike, gamble
with dice, smoke and spit with a hoarse
and grainy vigour. I will smell that note
in your sweat, you will eye the shadows
of my blouse and we will make love
on the stone flags, on the dirt of the yard,
until dusk falls, salt stiffens on cooling skin,
and the cicadas sing and sing until death.

Home Safe

She feels his skin, his stubbly hair, touches him
as she's dreamt of touching him through months
of not listening to the morning news, to any news

in case of roadside bombs or choppers down.
But now it's fatted calf and sex and visits from the in-laws,
sweet normality of getting in the shopping and trips to B&Q,

he remarks how small and light their car is.
These weeks she can't stop touching him,
fingertips to his hand, his thigh, to check

he's here, he's really here, home safe.
The weeks she thinks she has him back,
when his smell, his tread on the stairs, are golden

fog she doesn't see through – the marvel of his shoes
by the door and his toothbrush in the bathroom.
Before the patches of time when he isn't here

his gaze sliding over the windows, her face.
At night, she reaches out and he's not there
he's up, on patrol, checking the locks,

one night she wakes to find his hand above her mouth
checking she's still breathing.
She rings help-lines, rings doctors,

she wants to travel into darkness, bring him up
but she can't follow him, can't see him there
sees instead herself in the hall mirror

sitting on the floor, sobbing into the phone
he's not here, Mum, he's not really here.

Charlotte Wetton

Bident

I

He does not codify our bodies with his recipes
melons, plums, losing your cherry, but his hands
with the little white scars from the knife
and the burn mark across the palm, portion
and consume, shoulder, ribs and heart.

II

I like a mopped floor gleaming
so new you can't walk on it

the smell of baking and Ajax that says
job done, the hours are hospital cornered.

But some late nights I sprawl
in the freezer's cold embrace

eat ice-cream out the tub,
limbs trailing on the kitchen floor.

III

I think he would prefer a statue-woman
marble flesh, white and cool
who would gather coats at the door, softly
over her arms, like the wings of birds.

JESSICA WOOD

Jessica is entering into her final year of university after spending a year studying in Jamaica. She has been writing poetry for around 5 years after joining a writing group whilst at college in Sheffield. Heritage, diversity, class, gender and race are continuous markers in her life and consequently find themselves in her writing, see more at jessicalouisewood.co.uk or @jesslouwood on twitter.

Dorveille:
'there is nothing small about the small hours' – John Burnside

Open your eyes to 'the watch'
at 2am, then 3 then 4
squeeze your eyes tighter,
sigh a little louder, wrap the duvet
tighter and tighter,
let your sleep prowl, claim territory of your mind

Or open your eyes to dorveille,
a window of wandering minds
from 2 till 4 am.
Make use of sleeplessness+
write letters into poems that the day has no time for
interpret dreams so they no longer plague you
visit neighbours who you see, but never sit with
have sex, in what was thought the best time to conceive
or the conversations put off in daylight
then after, eyes droop in to natural stupor,
and in the gentle way that the moon and darkness
overtake the sun, sleep prowls over you.

Fragments

Not knowing a difference between love and knowledge,
she collected the sayings of people,
the movement of their limbs under stress and under joy.
The rise, pitch and crescendo of their voice in laughter
the loud and brash tenderness with which they speak to a mother,
and the shy words of affection to a lover.
She saw the determined selection of an earring to slip into a pierced lobe,
quiet evenings under duvets with nose in a book, bowing in a kind of prayer.
And so knowing how they like their tea or coffee in the morning,
knowing how to raise a smile, how to start the tongue rolling
in passionate verse, means that she knows how to love well.

YUAN YANG

Sichuan-born and Yorkshire-raised, Yuan is a correspondent for the *Financial Times* in Beijing, where she writes about the Chinese economy, the technology industry, housing and finance. She co-founded a charity, now head-quartered in Manchester, called Rethinking Economics (www.rethinkeconomics.org), which campaigns to change economics education around the world. Yuan has an MSc in Economics from the London School of Economics and a BA in Philosophy, Politics and Economics from Balliol College, Oxford.

Silk shirt

She picked me for her first airplane ride.
My colours were good for the arrival gate.
My silk wicked away the sweat of travel
and the anxiety of opened passports –

I came to absorb different tastes
to the ones I had come with.
She hung me damp on a wooden rack
that lifted like a trick into the ceiling
of her Manchester kitchen.
The murmuring wok underneath
raised shimmers of oil to line my hems.

I don't know how she always managed
to find clothes-hangers
while moving each season.
Never questioning, I went under
her folds and rinses and came
to rest in vacated closets.

I hardly saw that she grew older.
I was well rested, so stayed much similar.
One day, her younger self
took me for an airplane ride,
thinking my colours
would identify her
on the other side –

Dog Eat Dog

From the next room my grandpa declared:
"Capitalism is dog eat dog,"

a sentence left hanging
at my twelve-year-old face;

I was ahead in school
back home. I was worldly wise.
He was sixty-four. A famine,
a pension, and this granddaughter

who couldn't speak the dialect.
I turned the dogs over
in my mind. They were white with
black spots and were nuzzling one another.

I had come to expect
someone to greet me
at the end of every long-haul flight.
Who would recall themselves as familiar.
Who I had no choice but to accept.

I didn't worry about strangers.
I worried about snakes by the hill path
in the sizzling hum of the night.

The man with an inky
bruise on his leg told me
it was his fault really
for stumbling into their nest:
they only bite when they're scared.
Dogs, however –

– there were no tame ones in the village.
Nobody would've given good meat

to keep such things alive.

Yuan Yang

But where I grew up, they're pets or
companions. To be trusted with your life.
Unlike strangers at the station

who claim they're looking
for the same train compartment.
I would arrive through the gate
and wait for someone to call me

by my child name, which sounds like
little lamb, who follows her guide.
I wondered if my grandpa, then
was reprimanding me

for following the wrong ones.
But weren't you the one who handed me
through the customs line?
I cried then, but adults' minds are final.

Children are unfixed to a place
or a tongue or a time.
They are always ready
for a new lullaby:

yes, the summer was high –
my mama was good looking,
and my father – the state – would provide.

Routine

When I am infatuated with a person or place:
I am present
queuing
        at the tax office for a rental receipt,
I take in the dappled sunshine, the collection of
tiny pots of cacti, succulents that the cashiers are growing atop a stash of white
foamboard in the corner, the middle-aged
spread and how they are all women.
I keep filling the form in wrong
and they keep giving it back to me.

I leave thinking I have experienced
something.
        I am always ready
for the first time. Like watching your back
at the elevator door, the box full of
packing-foam flowers on my new floor,
the line at the airport, the daily mundane
that speaks of more, each morning I raise
my daily loaf:
        repeated, unique, unspectacular.

WARDA YASSIN

Warda is an EAL English tutor at a Sheffield school and a recreational poet at night. She loves the works and words of Warsan Shire, Hannah Lowe and Chimamanda Ngozi Adichie. She has performed alongside the likes of Buddy Wakefield, Jean Binta Breeze and Hollie McNish.

My sisters

have given me an insult-proof vest.
They shot me first, gifting me with armour
against the sting of others' words.
Now I'm immune to the insults of the universe.
Ayan cares for nothing,
Zuhur is unbeaten at scoffing,
Ikram taught me about plotting,
so my secrets are spoilt with options.
Each has advice, purple, green and orange.
My sisters would have been my friends
long before God intervened with blood.
They remind me to release my forked tongue,
to reject calls when they're in the wrong.
They are unruly teachers,
with lessons in how to grow.
They assure my soul
it is the best they know.

The Hijab

The hijab; my ethereal coat,
my divine ordained cloak.
Wallahi, the feeling it evokes.
No worldly words
can do it justice.
The hijab; my bespoke first expression,
slandered as quote unquote – 'oppression'.
Wallahi the feeling it evokes
is freefalling freedom at its most.
No aloof slurs
can make me go back to before
the hijab; my connection to the first
and foremost. My reminder
to remind myself before I talk.
These words will indicate
how another person reciprocates.
Show them you are the same –
it is who you are first.

Making Lips

When I was fuchsia pink lipstick,
I was always in your pocket
drowning in bus tickets and fluff,
being used by people
who didn't care enough.
At weddings, I would be
smeared geisha on top of liner,
in the hope of making lips
plusher and finer,
beaming from looks,
and all the while wishing
I was something real,
reflecting sunrays and moonlight
that made the wearer appreciate
the art of her lips,
their divine mission –
to speak first,
not to be kissed.

RUTH YATES

Ruth lives in Sheffield where she is studying speech and language therapy. Four times winner of the Foyle Young Poets Award, her poems have been shortlisted for an Eric Gregory Award and have appeared in *Cadaverine*, *Route 57*, *Mslexia*, Writing Squad booklet and *The North*.

Strawberries

When her cats died,
she buried them in plant pots.

They are in the sitting room
under the strawberry plants.

When I went to see her,
she offered me strawberries.

They were large, red.
She put cream on.

We sat there, growing whiskers
in the sun, holding claws.

I took the strawberries
home in green tupperware,

told you what I'd seen
and you laughed about all those cats.

One was born in 1994.

Bird Gift

I give you this bird,
so fat and so sweet,
so that when you aren't looking at it,
you'll keep the image
of the image of the bird.
A spider suspended in nothing
between two sunflowers,
remembers deep inside
its ancestral print
the looming bird,
and it shivers in the nothing,
but gets on with life
nevertheless,
the image of the bird
sunk in the tiny lakes of other dreams.

I give you this bird.
It sings somewhere else.
Its image is quiet,
fragment of wing and
feather.
Don't worry about
understanding it.

Playing in the Snow

Soft snow, tastes of bracken.
I gave you the full version of
Stopping by Woods on a Snowy Evening
but forgot the line *These woods are lovely,
dark and deep.* Remembered the promises,
the journey.

Later we played a game –
took it in turns to make footprints,
jumping with both feet,
strides, leaps,
hops.
Tiny steps and
                sweeping
                              elliptical steps
that crossed our legs into tangles.

The snow was deep.
The other person watched,
remembered, then followed.

The sun through the white glow of tree.
The wild boar and then the wolf
track, going the other way.
All the tiny bird brushing
feet.

The tree shadows stretched across the path,
all the way to L'Aquila.

Ruth Yates

Index of poems & first lines

23 June ... 17

123 Cherry Tree Lane ... 78

A Boy is a Gun ... 21

Acknowledgments ... 132

Aeolian Processes ... 97

After the first time, ... 11

Amber ... 64

Ancestors ... 94

A picture of dad pointing ... 78

A Scenic Moment ... 71

At the beginning of the world the moon was yawned ... 97

Autumn in New Jersey ... 15

A word that eats itself. ... 54

Before I was possible, ... 63

Beside the old Nile Apep handled the chaos ... 49

Bident ... 118

Bird Gift ... 129

Cancer ... 42

Celia and Rosalind ... 100

Christina Crashes The Wedding ... 45

Christopher ... 30

Close to midnight, we finish the first puzzle ... 16

Coal ... 63

Coming from the Mill ... 16

Crisis ... 110

Daily devotion ... 65

David, I don't feel like kissing tonight. ... 17

Dawn ... 93

Deliveroo ... 23

Deutsch ... 36
Dog Eat Dog ... 122
Dog Violets ... 40
Dorveille: ... 119
Do you remember to eat your five-a-day? ... 82
Eden ... 49
Enough Water To Drown ... 58
Everything is so divided where the sun's cut off ... 34
everything will be different. ... 116
Expedition ... 77
First, ochre your fingertips, and quaff helium. ... 103
First piece of advice: forget instincts. ... 105
Five-a-day ... 82
Flora ... 33
Fragments ... 120
Fragments/Campari ... 47
From the next room my grandpa declared: ... 122
From the sour breath of quarry towns we came, ... 94
Galatea ... 26
Gannet ... 70
Gaps ... 34
Glass ... 115
Glaukós ... 39
Going ... 50
Grandma's Kitchen ... 79
Halfhead ... 41
have given me an insult-proof vest. ... 125
He dies while crossing the stage ... 84
He does not codify our bodies with his recipes ... 118
He drew me up from the water. When drowning, ... 26
Here in the home of smoke and smog, my hometown grey, ... 96
He stayed in our flat for three months. ... 46

High Noon ... 20
His skin went patchwork red from smoke. ... 47
Hitching ... 105
Home ... 81
Home ... 109
Home Safe ... 117
How do you know if they're the one? ... 73
How to Prepare for Bad News ... 103
How To: Romance ... 72
I am in love with reversal. How a room is just a moor ... 19
I catch you in the post office, ... 114
I didn't fit the fish crates set out for me ... 40
I died. It was that simple. ... 53
I don't like church ... 110
I examine the artefacts, meticulously preserved. ... 80
I feel older in the evening, ... 43
If I'm left alone ... 109
I give you this bird, ... 129
I like how he says she is nothing   and does not mean her body ... 44
In another life ... 53
In another life they'd say she asked for it. ... 112
Index of poems & first lines ... 135
In Mexico ... 116
Instead of You Here ... 52
Introduction X ... 19
in which I am one of those born ... 107
In your absence I have had to make do with the simplest ... 52
In your bath you were naked, ... 42
I only want your half head ... 41
I Saw Myself ... 114
I scrub my feet in grandma's bathtub ... 68

I shoot along smooth tarmac ... 23
I stand, thigh deep in hurricane water, murky from home foundations
 churned into soup. ... 75
it has come, here, in Castle Market ... 22
I think very often of our moments that night ... 33
It is hard to have a scenic moment on a park bench ... 71
It's beautiful because   it's not sexual ... 35
It's true, sometimes ... 20
It was a brutal blue morning, not a soul ... 93
I used to be part of a team ... 115
I wanted Boyfriends who were good at Science. ... 108
I was walking up Northumberland Road, ... 24
I watch you through a fog ... 79
Judgement ... 111
Kissing the geographer ... 59
Landscape without Reiver ... 101
Lay your foundation – ... 65
   Lingering now for a house party – *You're all* ... 38
makes me feel like strawberries ... 12
Making Lips ... 127
Merrie City ... 96
Monday on Saturday ... 25
My sisters ... 125
Nightmare ... 90
Notes on missing a person ... 37
Not knowing a difference between love and knowledge, ... 120
Occupation ... 102
of a Salesman ... 84
Oh but come and chat out of the little sewing box! ... 36
Oh, they will try to keep it from you. ... 18
Old rain ... 48
One night last summer ... 14

Open your eyes to 'the watch' ... 119
Ordinary Durham Lad, hauled up ... 104
Oysters ... 43
Parliament, Fallen ... 67
Playing in the Snow ... 130
Pneumatophore ... 75
Polycystic ... 66
Popsicle ... 51
Possibly ... 57
Psychosomatic ... 54
Put in Longtown and Langholm and fill with egg ... 101
Recurring Dream ... 107
Romance ... 12
Routine ... 124
Sarah Good ... 99
Saturday, it's time to grow up. ... 25
School ... 108
She feels his skin, his stubbly hair, touches him ... 117
She fills the bath with just enough water. ... 58
She is invited because she'd be noticed more by her absence than her presence ... 45
She must have wished they were right in the end, ... 99
She picked me for her first airplane ride. ... 121
Shower ... 35
Silk shirt ... 121
Soft snow, tastes of bracken. ... 130
So, I turned to lens cutting for a living. ... 102
Some Of Us Do Not Have Freckles ... 68
Sonnet – house party ... 38
Spacemen ... 76
Standing in the light with you is ... 30
St Chad ... 104

Strange, how over and over again the west is won. ... 21
Strawberries ... 128
Take off your shoes, he said ... 77
The autumns of my childhood are best: ... 15
The Bat ... 32
The continuity of substance ... 73
The crows are lifting off like black film, peeling. ... 60
The Far Side of the Moon ... 113
The father inside my freezer shivers ... 51
The fens were frozen clean over this morning, ... 62
The First Five Storms ... 87
The girls who bullied me at school ... 48
The Girl Who Lived in a House Made of Books ... 55
The girl who lives in the house made of books ... 55
The Hijab ... 126
The hijab; my ethereal coat, ... 126
The Minute of Vision ... 22
Then, hollows and jutting out bits – ... 113
The night I am in close trapping air ... 39
The Occupant ... 46
The Owl ... 24
'There,' he says, pointing, 'there, see?' ... 13
There is a dead mole outside my ... 50
these are not the wings ... 32
These spacemen lying down ... 76
The Visit ... 14
This is his body   written for me ... 37
this is the ugliest bed i've / ever slept in. i take black and white / ... 90
this is what it feels like ... 69
To a Back, 2am ... 91
Train poem ... 60

Tsukumogami* ... 18
Ultrasound shows them: ... 66
Umma's Room ... 80
under fierce sunlight ... 64
Ursa Major ... 112
Vivian ... 11
was best. His mouth folded up ... 59
Wax and Water ... 28
We can afford to know nothing ... 67
We sat up late one night to watch the sky ... 87
We spent our days on the phone together ... 111
When her cats died, ... 128
When I am infatuated with a person or place: ... 124
When I see my house from the train, ... 81
When I was fuchsia pink lipstick, ... 127
White flash against the ... 70
Winter poem ... 62
Wives and Girlfriends ... 44
Wolf ... 13
You might have seen me, walking, ... 57
Your back ... 91
Your cells collapse ... 28
you wear clouds inside out ... 69
You were the kind of nice you see in the cinema: ... 72
You, whose company I cannot live out of. ... 100

Acknowledgments

Helen Bowell

'Coming from the Mill' was published in Issue 17 of The Manchester Review

Imogen Cassels

'The Bat' first appeared in *Ambit* #222
'Christopher' and 'Flora' both appeared online at *The Literateur*.

Jenny Danes

'Gaps', 'Deutsch', 'Shower' and 'Notes on a missing person' were published in the pamphlet *Gaps* (smith|doorstop, 2017)
'Gaps' was published in *The North* issue 56.
'Deutsch' and 'Shower' were published in *The Rialto* issue 88.
'Notes on missing a person' was highly commended in the Bridport Prize 2016.

James Giddings

'Instead of you here' first appeared in Magma.
'Popsicle' and 'Instead of You Here' were published in the pamphlet *Everything is Scripted* (Templar, 2016).

Sarah Gonnet

'The Girl who Lives in a House Made of Books' was previously published in the Writing Squad's magazine *Push*.
'Psychosomatic' was published in the pamphlet *Voices* (Survivor's Press, 2017).

Katherine Henderson

'Daily Devotion' was first published on *Foxglove Journal*, February 2017.

Katherine Horrex

'Parliament, Fallen' was previously published in the *Morning Star*
'Polycystic' won second prize in the MCR Global Health Poetry Competition.

Theophilus Kwek

'The First Five Storms' as a set was first published in a pamphlet of the same name (smith|doorstop, 2017); sections have been previously published in *THINK Journal*, *The Missing Slate*, and the *Somerville Arts Festival*.

Dominic Leonard

'To a Back' first appeared in *Cherwell*.

Fielding Ronshaugen

'Sarah Good' was previously published in the Writing Squad's magazine *Push*.

Alexander Shaw

'How to Prepare for Bad News' was Commended in the Christopher Tower Poetry Competition 2014.

'Landscape without Reiver' has appeared in *Ash Magazine* (Oxford University Poetry Society, Michaelmas 2014).

'Occupation' was published in *The London Magazine*, October/November 2016.

Jasmine Simms

'St Chad' first appeared in *The Palatinate*.

'Recurring Dream' and 'Hitching' first appeared in *All That's Ever Happened* (The Poetry School)

'School' first appeared in *Magma*

Charlotte Wetton

'In Mexico', 'Bident' and 'Home Safe' were published in the pamphlet *I Refuse to Turn into a Hatstand* (Calder Valley Poetry, 2017).

'Bident' was published in *Stand*, Spring 2015.

'Home Safe' won the Poetry Business Yorkshire Prize in the 2016 pamphlet competition judged by Billy Collins, and appeared in *The North*.

Ruth Yates

'Strawberries' and 'Playing in the snow' have previously appeared in *The North*.